To John

Xmas 1980

STEAM LOCOMOTIVES
OF THE
EAST AFRICAN RAILWAYS

David & Charles Locomotive Studies

Locomotive Monographs

General Editor:

O. S. Nock, BSc, CEng, FICE, FIMechE

Class EC3 4–8–4 + 4–8–4 No 5813 pounds uphill with a goods train on the Nairobi-Nakuru line in September 1972

DAVID & CHARLES LOCOMOTIVE STUDIES

STEAM LOCOMOTIVES OF THE EAST AFRICAN RAILWAYS

R. RAMAER

DAVID & CHARLES
NEWTON ABBOT LONDON
NORTH POMFRET (VT) VANCOUVER

0 7153 6437 5

Published in the United States of America
by David & Charles Inc
North Pomfret Vermont 05053 USA

Published in Canada
by Douglas David & Charles Limited
3645 McKechnie Drive West Vancouver BC

Set in 10 on 11 point Plantin
and printed in Great Britain
for David & Charles (Holdings) Limited
South Devon House Newton Abbot Devon

CONTENTS

PREFACE

EXACTLY eighty years ago, in 1893, during the heyday of the colonial era, work started on the first East African railway in what was then German East Africa; this line, the Usambara Eisenbahn, began at the port of Tanga and ran northwest with the idea of connecting the then relatively well developed coastal area with the region around Lake Victoria. It was soon followed by a second line, this time in British-controlled territory for in 1896, work started on the Uganda Railway from Mombasa, about a hundred miles north of Tanga, also to Lake Victoria, to connect Uganda with the Indian Ocean. A third line followed the earlier two in 1905, again on German soil, the present Central Line of Tanzania from Dar es Salaam to Kigoma on Lake Tanganyika.

By coincidence, both systems were built to metre gauge, although the Uganda Railway was initially planned as 3ft 6in, and this circumstance later allowed both systems to be integrated into one internationally coherent network. The administrative merger took place in 1948, when Kenya-Uganda Railways & Harbours and Tanganyika Railways & Port Services were amalgamated into East African Railways & Harbours Administration. This, finally, was split up in 1969 into East African Railways Corporation and East African Harbours Corporation.

Motive power development began in the 1890s with a handful of quite modest locomotives, both on the British and German lines. In the case of the Uganda Railway, the first engines were taken over from railways in British India and development went on to culminate eventually in the mightiest steam locomotives ever built for the metre gauge. Much of this steam power is still in operation today, an increasingly rare thing in the late twentieth century, and it is scheduled to be so until 1976. After then, diesel traction, not introduced until the 1950s, will take over fully and although a fair number of diesels have already made their appearance on the EAR network, at the time of writing about sixty per cent of the total stock consists of steam engines.

Little information has been available in the past on the locomotives of pre–1914 German East Africa, apart from a limited number of sources published in German. Details of makers' numbers, besides other relevant data, have been included wherever possible, to obtain as complete a picture as practicable. In two cases this proved particularly difficult, because the Uganda Railway obtained a number of second-hand engines from India, as did the Tanganyika Railway in later years, and in the case of the German engines many records were lost. This, and the fact that many once well known builders have gone out of business, has resulted in some unavoidable gaps.

Despite today's tendency to convert to the metric system, the familiar imperial measurements have been retained in this book, except in the case of the German engines, which were built to metric standards

During the preparation of the manuscript, I have received a great deal of assistance from various sources and I wish to thank staff members of East African Railways for their help. My special thanks are due to the chief mechanical engineer, Mr J. Mimano, and to Messrs P. D. Swan, assistant chief mechanical engineer, J. F. Phillipson, mechanical engineer motive power, N. G. Hedges, shedmaster at Nairobi and F. Jordan, onetime loco inspector, for their unstinting help and encouragement.

I am also indebted to the Crown Agents for its invaluable assistance especially concerning the older locomotive types on both the UR/KUR and the TR, and to Dipl Ing H. Schroeter for his advice and kind permission to use material and photographs from his book on the railways on the former German protectorates in Africa, thus enabling me to give a substantially more complete picture of German East Africa than would otherwise have been possible. Valuable assistance, too, was given by Mr W. E. Bulman, former chief mechanical engineer of the EAR, the Mitchell Library in Glasgow, the Railway Industry Association and various locomotive builders, all of which is gratefully acknowledged.

Nairobi, 1973   R. RAMAER

9

FOREWORD

I AM pleased to have the opportunity of introducing this book on East African Railways (and its predecessors) steam locomotives, and to commend Mr Ramaer, the author, for his enthusiasm and effort in compiling the information for his book, particularly concerning the former separate Uganda Railway and Tanganyika Railway. Mr Ramaer approached me almost two years ago with the suggestion that a book on the locomotives in East Africa should be written, and the idea appealed to me as no other complete written material on the subject existed. I was therefore more than willing to provide encouragement and support to Mr Ramaer in locating what information and detail could be found among old records in railway headquarters, and from long serving employees in the mechanical engineering department of the railway.

This book includes details of all the steam locomotives which have been in service in East Africa during the last seventy-five years, and since the inception of a railway system in East Africa. I am sure it will prove of great interest to steam locomotive enthusiasts throughout the world, and it will also form a most useful reference book for railways in general and for anyone undertaking research on the subject.

The East African Railways serves the three partner states of Kenya, Uganda and Tanzania and has existed for only twenty-five years. Before 1948, two separate systems existed, the Kenya-Uganda Railways and Harbours and the Tanganyika Railways and Ports Services, which amalgamated to form the East African Railways & Harbours; in 1969 this organisation was split into the present form of two separate corporations, the East African Railways and East African Harbours.

Originally the Uganda Railway, as it was then called although it only passed through Kenya, was built by the British commencing from Mombasa in 1896, and track laying reached Nyrobi three years later on 30 May 1899. As the country ahead presented heavier earthworks for a railway than had been experienced crossing the Athi Plains, and ample space with level ground and a fairly good water supply existed, the area was selected as a site for the principal workshops, and quickly developed

into the township of Nairobi. Today, after less than seventy-five years' existence, Nairobi is a modern city and is the site of the East African Railways headquarters.

The Uganda Railway eventually reached its destination at Port Florence, (now Kisumu), on the shores of Lake Victoria, in December 1901 after five-and-a-half years of toil and hardship, and the route to the Uganda Protectorate was completed by steamer over the lake.

The original Tanganyika Railway was built by the Germans, fortuitously also of metre gauge, the same as the Uganda Railway, but with other different technical features. The first line to be constructed was the Usambara Bahn, from Tanga towards Moshi, track laying commencing in May 1893; two years later only 28km had been built, by which time the private railway company's capital was exhausted and work stopped. The German Government then took over the project to develop the land alongside the alignment for growing sisal and rubber; in July 1899 work recommenced and the track reached Moshi by September 1911. The following year the Germans did the survey for the extension of the Tanga Line, at that time known as the Nordbahn, from Moshi to Arusha, but it was not actually built until 1927–9, and then by the British.

The Mittelland Bahn, (now the Central Line), was started from Dar es Salaam in February 1905; construction did not present the German surveyors and engineers with so many and such difficult engineering problems as had to be overcome by the British builders of the Uganda Railway from Mombasa to Port Florence. Nevertheless, similar climatic and labour problems were encountered, and the line did not reach Tabora until February 1912, and Kigoma on Lake Tanganyika two years later in February 1914. The standard of station buildings and structures for the railway was very high, and all the original stone-built stations are standing with little alteration to this day. Tabora became a large railway headquarters. The line from Tabora towards Mwanza was started in 1914 and its construction continued after the outbreak of World War I. The war prevented considerable rail expansion planned in Tanganyika and at the end of hostilities, by which time most of the bridges and rolling stock had been destroyed, German East Africa became Tanganyika Territory, administered by the British, under League of Nations mandate.

The history of these two pioneer railways and their successors, is covered in detail by Mr Ramaer in the following chapters, which present the subject in a very readable manner, and at the same time gives technical details of the locomotives. The director general of the East African Railways Corporation has been pleased to provide the majority of the photographs of locomotives for illustrating this book.

Since independence was achieved in 1961–3 by the three East African partner states, East African Railways has introduced diesel locomotives for main line working on a number of sections; complete dieselisation is planned within the next four years, by which time no steam locomotive will remain in service.

J. MIMANO
Chief Mechanical Engineer
East African Railways Corporation

Nairobi, Kenya
2 April 1973

CHAPTER 1

INTRODUCTION

THE history of railways in East Africa dates back to 1887, when British and German interests acquired rights on the East African mainland from Sultan Barghash of Zanzibar, who claimed territorial rights over the area. In the northern part of it, between the Umbe river and Kipini, the sultan ceded his powers to the British East Africa Association, which in the following year became the Imperial British East Africa Company. In the south, in the inland area of Tanganyika, a German protectorate was established in 1886, following the activities of a Dr Karl Peters, who concluded several treaties for Germany with local chiefs.

The Brussels Conference of 1889–90 decided upon the future of Central Africa and one of its recommendations was that the signatory powers were to take care that roads and railways were constructed to connect the area with the coast as well as to provide easy access to inland waters, among which the great lakes and the Congo and Nile rivers ranked first. The ultimate objective was to suppress the slave trade, still important in eastern Africa, and to allow for the development of legal trade. Article four authorised the signatory powers to delegate their commitments to chartered companies.

Britain did so and left much initiative to the Imperial British East Africa Company, which existed to develop the trade with Uganda. This company also built the first East African railway, a seven-mile 2ft gauge tramway from Mombasa inland, which received the impressive title of Central Africa Railway. It never possessed any locomotives, however, and was discontinued as soon as there appeared a chance for a more substantial railway. It was generally realised that such a railway would greatly facilitate the trade with

The track of the Central Africa Railway in the streets of Mombasa in the early 1890s

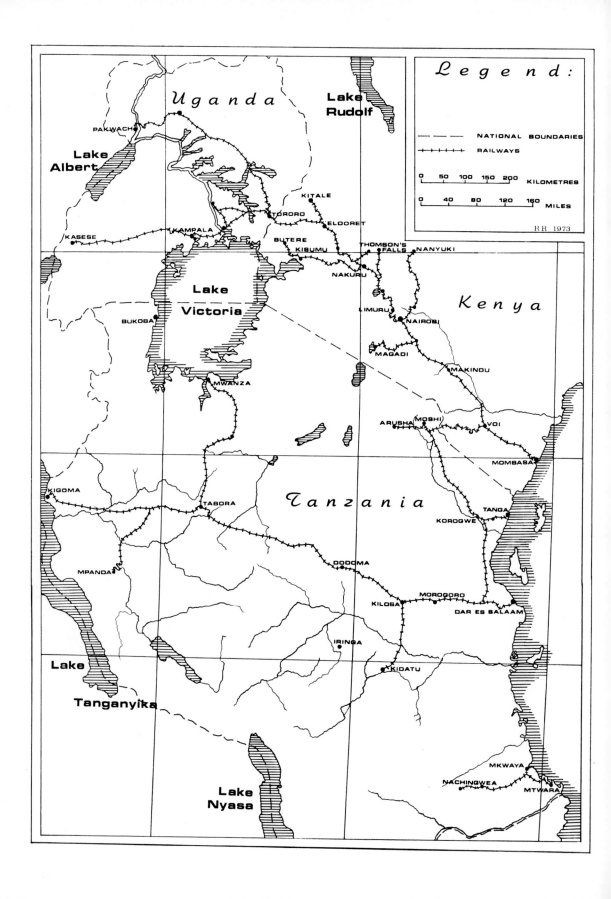

Uganda besides eliminating the slave trade, and several surveys were carried out in the 1890s to decide on the best possible route for such a railway. Building it would, however, by no means be a simple undertaking, as physical barriers in the landscape, health conditions, labour supply, the danger of wild animals, not to speak of the attitude of the local population, all needed attention.

The report of Captain MacDonald, who carried out a survey between December 1891 and September 1893, suggested a route of 657 miles from Mombasa to Lake Victoria at a total expense of £2,240,000 for a light railway, against £3,685,000 for a more substantial railway. The proposed gauge was 3ft 6in with steel sleepers and 50lb rail, while as most suitable locomotive type 'an enlarged version of F class metre-gauge engine used in India' was recommended, of which thirty were thought to be necessary. Even the lowest of these estimates went far beyond the financial capacities of the Imperial British East Africa Company and in 1894 the British Government took over the company's interests in East Africa. About the same time the Railway Bill, despite vigorous parliamentary opposition, was pushed forward and finally accepted. At that time, however, the 3ft 6in gauge decision had been changed to metre gauge to facilitate the procurement of rolling stock from India in case of emergency circumstances, a policy which has ever since been represented as a grave mistake.

While the Imperial British East Africa Company was in fact laying the foundations of what was to become British East Africa, Germany proceeded to expand her sphere of influence to include the coastal area as well. As a result of this policy, a rather tenuous political situation developed between the British and German governments which was only normalised by the Anglo-German agreement of 1890, whereby new spheres of influence were established along a borderline which marks the present Kenya-Tanzania border, from the coast inland to the then Congo Free State. Over this sphere of influence Germany declared on 1 January 1891 the protectorate of Deutsch-Ostafrika or German East Africa, thereby placing it under direct government control from Berlin through a governor in Dar es Salaam.

In this newly established protectorate, the German colonial authorities made up their minds quicker than the British did in the north as far as railways were concerned and in the same year 1891, the Eisenbahn Gesellschaft für Deutsch-Ostafrika, or Railway Company for German East Africa, was established. Its somewhat vague goal was to build a railway from Tanga at the coast through the Usambara Mountains to Lake Victoria. In the view of colonial administration the Usambaras looked promising for development and agricultural settlement and were thus included in the projected rail connection. This line, work on which started in 1893, was not destined ever to reach the lake, however, as German rule in the area ended before the line was completed.

Independently, a second line was started in 1905 to run inland from Dar es Salaam to Kigoma on the eastern shore of Lake Tanganyika, reached in February 1914. This, the present Central Line of Tanzania, was variously referred to in German times as Ost-Afrikanische Eisenbahn Gesellschaft (OAEG), Ost-Afrikanische Centralbahn or Mittellandbahn. One of its aims was the transport of ores from the coppermines in Belgian-administered Katanga to the Indian Ocean, at a time when there was no direct rail connection available from Katanga to the Atlantic. As World War I broke out only six months after completion of the line, however, this idea never came to fruition in German times.

During the war both the Uganda Railway and the German lines were heavily stressed, and later in the war the latter were systematically destroyed by the retreating German army. After the war, both German lines became the Tanganyika Railway. The Uganda Railway became Kenya-Uganda Railway (KUR) in February 1926, when the system was being extended to Uganda proper by the Nakuru-Eldoret-Tororo-Kampala line. This opened up the highlands of the Uasin Gishu Plateau west of the Great Rift Valley, the 'White Highlands', and was therefore initially known as the Uasin Gishu Railway (UGR). This name disappeared when the line reached Uganda proper, becoming the through line to connect Uganda with the coast and doing away with the cumbersome change to lake steamer at Kisumu. In Tanganyika, the intended German line from Tabora to Ruanda-Urundi was diverted to Mwanza, and the Tanga Line was extended from Moshi to Arusha (1929). Further activity was stopped by the depression.

In the field of locomotive operation, the KUR went in for big engines, standardising the 4-8-2 + 2-8-4 Garratt for heavy mixed traffic from 1926 onwards, and in 1939 even introducing the 4-8-4 + 4-8-4. The generally easier-graded lines in Tanganyika acquired mainly conventional eight-coupled locomotives, only one Garratt class being introduced in 1931.

Shortly after 1945 the railway picture changed

considerably compared with the 1930s; the TR system was extended by two important lines, the first of which was a connection between the Tanga Line and the Central Line. The second was in the southern part of the country, near the Moçambique border, where the Southern Province Railway was built from the port of Mtwara inland, intended to handle traffic for the groundnuts scheme. The latter, however, was a total failure and the SPR disappeared with it, being dismantled in the early 1960s. On the KUR, the last important network expansion included both the Northern and Western Uganda Extensions, built during the 1950s. In the last twenty years have also come political changes and the independence of most African countries. Tanganyika became known as Tanzania but Kenya and Uganda retained their former names.

Shortly after World War II, talks started on the integration of the two railway systems, and this led to the formation of the East African Railways & Harbours on 1 May 1948. After about twenty years, in 1969, EAR & H was again split into two separate corporations, East African Railways and East African Harbours. East African Railways officially celebrated its 75th anniversary in 1971, starting from the beginning of the Uganda Railway in 1896. However, the Tanga Line in Tanzania is older, work having begun in 1893, and it would therefore have been more appropriate if the corporation had celebrated its 80th birthday in 1973. This seems the right moment to look back at the development of motive power during these eighty years, which is certainly as interesting as any on a narrow-gauge network in the world.

CHAPTER 2

DEUTSCH-OSTAFRIKA, 1893-1914

THE TANGA LINE

(Eisenbahn Gesellschaft für Deutsch-Ostafrika-Usambara Eisenbahn, later called Ostafrikanische Nordbahn).

IN German East Africa, preparatory work on the intended railway from Tanga to Lake Victoria started at Tanga in 1891; initial surveys were carried out and the route fixed on Tanga, Moshi, Arusha and south of Mount Kilimanjaro to the west, to reach the lake somewhere near Mwanza. Track laying started in June 1893 from Tanga. Rails of 15½kg/m, or about 31lb/yd were used in conjunction with wooden sleepers, but the latter in their original condition, proved a delicacy for local termites, and even more so having been shipped to Germany and back for treatment. The German engineers had not yet had an opportunity to gain tropical experience and this was the first real difficulty encountered. Sleepers were changed to steel, but there were other difficulties: steel poles of considerable length had to be used to make the telegraph line wildlife-proof and such animals as elephants and giraffes required poles about 30ft high!

Construction proceeded slowly, frequently, because of narrow surveying, unsuitable alignments were chosen for the route, the line and engines were not kept in good repair, and much of the earlier eastern line section was built in a generally indifferent and unsatisfactory manner.

These setbacks caused the private railway company to go bankrupt after only a few years, when the line had proceeded no further than Muheza, only 40km from Tanga, and it was not until 1899, when the German Reich acquired the line and all its equipment from the Eisenbahn Gesellschaft für Deutsch-Ostafrika (EGFDOA), that work continued towards Korogwe, Buiko and Mombo, which was reached in February 1905. This work was done by the then well known contracting firm Lenz & Co through its subsidiary the Deutsche Kolonial Eisenbahn Bau- und Betriebs Gesellschaft, (DKEBBG) the German Colonial Railway Building and Operating Company. The DKEBBG made a good job of its part of the line which was vastly superior to the Tanga-Korogwe section. It was laid with 20kg/m rail on steel sleepers. Good economic returns enabled the contractors to build the line to Moshi, to which place traffic began on 7 February 1912. Finance had been allocated to continue the line to Arusha, but the outbreak of World War I stopped the work. In altered form it was eventually carried out during the British mandate period in 1929. Plans dated November 1913 envisaged the extension of the line from Arusha to either Mwanza or Speke Gulf, but this did not materialise.

Apart from the Usambara Eisenbahn, there was a privately-owned 750mm gauge line from Tengeni, 43km from Tanga, to Sigi, a distance of 23·6km. Sigi was the rail connection for a lumbering company, the Deutsche Holzgesellschaft für Ostafrika, as well as a biological-agricultural research station at Amani, about three miles further on. For this line, two six-coupled tank locomotives were supplied by Orenstein & Koppel of Berlin. This manufacturer had standardised on the construction of such lightweight engines, and various four- and six-coupled types were available from stock. Both the Sigi locomotives were 0–6–0 tanks but of different power output, and consequently tractive effort was not identical. The heavier of the two had an output equivalent to 50hp. As they were bought from stock, the author has been unable to trace their works numbers, but both were probably built in 1910. The line was operated by the separate Sigi Eisenbahn Gesellschaft (SEG) or Sigi Railway Company, which was fully owned by the lumbering company. The Sigi railway opened to traffic in 1911, but suffered financial trouble during German ownership and even more so after the

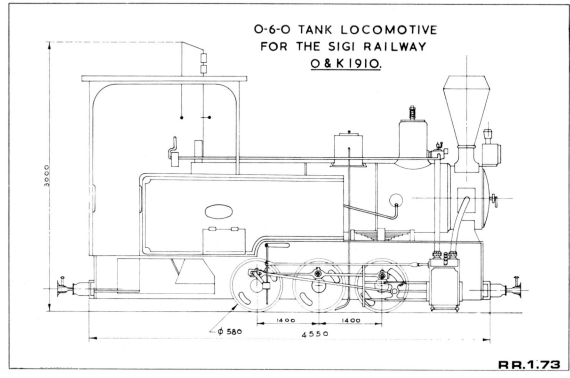

Drawing 1: 0–6–0 tank locomotive for the Sigi Railway

UE engine No 2, an 0–4–2T built by Vulcan Stettin in 1893

UE engine No 1 with an early passenger train ready for departure at Tanga station

war; consequently it was closed from 2 January 1924. Nothing is known with certainty about the ultimate fate of the two locomotives, but, presumably, they came to an end under the breaker's torch.

The first engines to be used on the Tanga Line itself were five 0–4–2 tank locomotives, built in 1893 by Vulcan of Stettin. They belonged to a fairly widely used type of Lokalbahn locomotive for Vulcan had virtually standardised these locomotives into a few well defined types for branch lines and light railways in Germany itself. These locomotives were wood burners and were used mainly for line building and shunting purposes when the railway had grown beyond its initial few miles' length. Originally, they were used on passenger trains as well.

Rising traffic loads, however, led the Usambara Eisenbahn (UE) to look for something more substantial and in 1900 Jung supplied five compound Mallet 0–4–4–0Ts as numbers 1–5, later renumbered 6–10. The Mallet principle represented a solution often chosen in those days to obtain a locomotive with sufficient tractive effort but without the disadvantage of a long coupled-wheelbase,

as in the case of a rigid-frame locomotive of comparable size and power. The adverse effects of higher maintenance cost and lower adhesion factor than that of a comparable eight-coupled locomotive had to be accepted with this configuration. To provide enough space for the firebox and ashpan, the rigid high-pressure part, comprising the third and fourth axles, had outside frames, whereas the low-pressure part had inside frames. These engines also carried names, in this case of the different German states, a rather uncommon practice on the German lines.

At a later stage the line was improved, the minimum curve radius being increased to more than 200m, and eight-coupled locomotives with rigid frames made their appearance. Four tank locomotives with a 2–8–0T wheel arrangement were built for the UE by Messrs Orenstein & Koppel in 1908 to a standardised tank engine design used on all German colonial railways in Africa for either metre or 3ft 6in gauge, as in the case of South West Africa. They were a distinct improvement over the Mallets. Although they were designed to burn coal, the high price of imported coal meant that they remained on wood fuel, which

19

UE Mallet 0–4–4–0T No 8 with a passenger train at Mombo

must have given trouble with fireboxes and ash-pans.

An even bigger stride forward was made for the last locomotives to be received by the Usambara-Eisenbahn, a class of four 2–8–0 tender engines. Two were built by Orenstein & Koppel in 1910 and two more in 1912, running numbers 15–18. Their introduction resulted from heavier and longer trains to be worked over longer distances, now that the line had grown beyond its initial stages. On these long journeys adhesive weight was inevitably reduced en route as water and fuel were used and the inherently restricted bunker capacity of the tank engines, even with auxiliary tenders for fire-wood and water, had become troublesome.

With coupled wheels of 1000mm and pony wheels of 700mm, the wheel diameters of the tender engines were standardised with those of the tanks, but the absence of side tanks had allowed greater use of the permissible seven ton axle loading which resulted in a bigger boiler and substantially increased tractive effort. The firebox was placed on the frame plates resulting in a high-pitched boiler, drive was on the third coupled axle, and the cylin-

ders were fitted with slide valves built under one casing integral with the cylinder instead of in a separate box on the cylinder casing as was the usual German practice. The steam bell and sand box on top of the boiler also helped to give them an appearance that differed markedly from what was to become normal on the Tanga Line in later years.

These 2–8–0s were the last German locomotives to be built for the UE and they brought the total of available engines up to eighteen. With this stock, traffic continued until well into the war.

THE CENTRAL LINE
(Ost Afrikanische Eisenbahn Gesellschaft, also variously called Ostafrikanische Centralbahn and Mittellandbahn)

ALREADY in 1891 plans were drawn up for an Ostafrikanische Centralbahn, to run inland from Dar es Salaam, from the previous year the capital of German East Africa. A few years later, the plans were revised, but it was not until 1904 that the Reichstag accepted the idea of the Ost Afrikanische

Eisenbahn Gesellschaft (OAEG), or East African Railway Company, almost the same title as is used by the present-day railway corporation.

Construction commenced in Dar es Salaam on 1 February 1905, by a private subcontractor Philipp Holzmann of Frankfurt am Main, a firm with international fame in railway building outside Europe. Taking into account the difficulties experienced with the Usambarabahn, the contractor started building with rails of 20kg/m (40·3lb/yd) on steel sleepers, and avoided gradients steeper than 1 in 40, which, however, resulted in the need to accept curves as sharp as 100m radius (300ft).

The first 21km to Pugu was ready in October 1906 and Morogoro (209km) was reached one year later. After about five years, traffic had increased so much that it became necessary to realign the very tight curves in the eastern sections of the line and to relay the track with rails of 27·8kg/m (55lb/yd), to allow for 10 tonne axle loadings. Further building went on without major difficulties, Tabora was reached in 1912 and from there work continued to Lake Tanganyika.

The crossing of the Malagarasi river, the descent into the Rift Valley and the subsequent climb uphill at the western edge presented engineering problems, but they were minor indeed in comparison to those which the Uganda Railway in the north had to surmount. The Central Line is in general much easier and the ruling gradient is limited to 1 in 40. Thus, Kigoma on the shore of Lake Tanganyika was reached on 1 February 1914, exactly nine years after work had begun in Dar es Salaam, and fourteen months ahead of contract time.

One problem was the limited availability of feedwater for the engines, and water supply stations and locomotive maintenance depots had to be built at regular 200km intervals. The first locomotives for the OAEG were four 0–4–0 tank engines, built by Henschel of Kassel; four more of the same type were supplied in 1909. They were intended primarily for the line building purposes and were always in service near the railhead. They could, however, be used for regular branch-line traffic and therefore possessed equipment for the continuous Hardy vacuum brake; later engines received the more modern Körting equipment.

In 1907, after four of these engines had been supplied, a fifth 0–4–0 tank was put in service. This engine was slightly different and also some years older than the earlier ones; it had been built in 1893 by an obscure manufacturer and was presumably taken over from the contractor Holzmann &

Engine No 2 of the OAEG with a line building train at Ugaga (now Malagarasi)

OAEG Mallet 0–4–4–0T No 24 with an engineering train in Malagarasi station

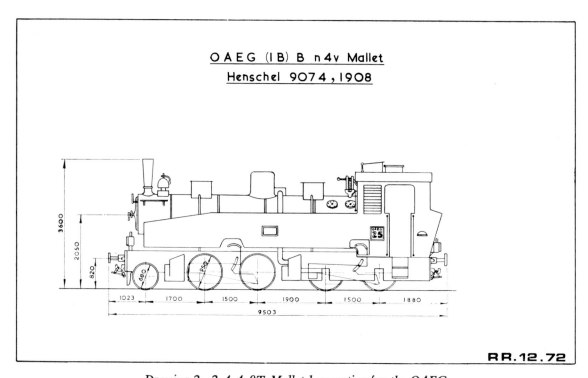

Drawing 2: 2–4–4–0T Mallet locomotive for the OAEG

OAEG 2–4–4–0T No 27 of the last Mallet class to be built for German East Africa

Co, but the author has been unable to trace further details.

A special feature of the early OAEG engines was that they could be used as both coal and oil burners, and the Henschel locomotives had a bunker capacity of $\frac{1}{2}$ ton of coal besides 300 litres (66 gallons) of fuel oil. Their water capacity was 2 m³ (440 gallons). These little engines had a comparatively long life, surviving the war and the subsequent change to British management, and the last did not go out of service before the early 1930s. The same considerations that governed the choice of Mallets by the Usambarabahn brought the OAEG to ordering five comparable Mallet 0–4–4–0Ts, four of which were supplied by Henschel in 1905 and put in service during the first half of 1906 with the fifth following in 1907; like the 0–4–0s they were built for either coal or oil fuel.

The problem with this type of engine was the restricted tractive effort and running was not satisfactory because of the lack of a leading pony truck, a rather common complaint with this type of locomotive. Therefore, Henschel supplied a second batch of four locomotives in 1908 as 2–4–4–0Ts with larger boilers and cylinders. They also had a higher working pressure of 14 atmospheres (at) (200lb/sq in) in comparison to 12at (170lb/sq in) for the earlier engines, while the bunker capacity had been increased from 1·2 to 2·2 tonnes of coal. Oil fuel had been discarded.

From its earliest days, the OAEG had experimented with the automatic MCB coupler, encouraged by satisfactory results on narrow-gauge lines in Thuringia. Several derailments, which no doubt could be debited to faulty track-laying rather than to the MCB couplers, partially brought the railway back to the old system of central buffer and screw coupling, although the MCBs were retained on some engines until the end of German times. The MCB was placed 850mm above rail level compared with 820mm for the buffer and screw coupling. The latter system was common to all German colonial railways in Africa; in East Africa, it was abolished with the beginning of British management.

The first sections of the Central Line had been built with some extremely tight curves of about 300ft radius, but when the line reached flatter country the minimum became more reasonable and it became possible for the OAEG to revert from the complex and expensive Mallets to rigid-frame locomotives. The Gölsdorf system allowed spring-controlled sideplay in coupled axles and thus eight-coupled engines were introduced on the line. The first solution tried was the 0–8–2 tank, built with the pony truck under the fuel bunker to make adhesion independent of diminishing supplies to the maximum possible extent, besides making riding somewhat more comfortable for the crew. High prices for imported coal from Europe had made the railway look for a cheaper alternative and these engines were the first to be built for wood fuel. Henschel supplied them in 1909 as works numbers 9301–2, running numbers 47–8.

OAEG Henschel 0–8–2T No 48 fitted with MCB couplers

Borsig-built 2–8–0 standard tank locomotive for the OAEG; by 1910 twenty-four of this type were in service

Simultaneously, Borsig and Orenstein & Koppel introduced an alternative and more logical solution in the shape of six 2–8–0T engines, also built for wood fuel. Both types, with only $5\frac{1}{2}$ and 5 cubic metres water capacity respectively, normally carried auxiliary tenders for both water and firewood, besides hoses on the engine to allow for taking water en route.

From this class and a comparable, but compound engine, supplied, also by Orenstein & Koppel, to South West Africa and Togo, a standardised 2–8–0T locomotive was developed, which was supplied to all German colonial lines in Africa. Besides serving on other railways, it worked on the Usambarabahn, as described above, and was built for the OAEG by Borsig, O & K, Hanomag (or Georg Egestorff, as this firm was originally known) and Maffei to a total of eighteen engines in 1909–10. Including the engines of the first batches by O & K and Borsig of six locomotives, the total of the *Einheitstenderlok* (standard tank locomotive) classes amounted to twenty-four engines by the end of German rule.

All the 2–8–0T locomotives had the same cylinders, except for the compounds, and, but for those in South West Africa, were wood burners. Running at speed was certainly better than in the case of the 0–8–2T a point of some importance when maximum speeds were raised to 45km/h, and planning envisaged 60km/h (36mph) for the Dar es Salaam-Kigoma mail trains.

The standard tanks were a good, straightforward design and were kept in service for a fairly long period under British management; the last ones even survived World War II, being withdrawn in 1951. A weak point, however, was their susceptibility to running hot axleboxes on the leading pony truck, a tendency which manifested itself especially during the later part of their careers.

The last and biggest Germans on the Tanganyikabahn were 2–8–0 tender locomotives, fifteen of which were supplied by Hanomag in 1911–12, with a further five in 1913; they were numbered 101–20. With a maximum service weight of 46·2 tonnes ($45\frac{1}{2}$ tons), 39·1 of which was adhesive they were taken in service only after the eastern sections of the line from Dar es Salaam to Morogoro had been relaid in 55lb rail, allowing ten tons axle load. The same rail was later used from Morogoro onwards to Kigoma.

On level lines, these engines handled 500-ton trains, and on 1 in 55 gradients 250 tons at 10 km/h. Three carried feedwater purifiers/preheaters on top of the boiler. In their day, for the narrow gauge, they were advanced locomotives, and in the early post-war years, enginemen commented favourably upon those that survived. Nevertheless, the fact that they were not in line with British engineering practices presumably was the reason that all were scrapped in the period between the wars. The first ones went in the early 1920s, but the last survived until 1937, where it was in use on the Mwanza line. Without doubt the bulk of the class disappeared much earlier than would have been the case if the line had continued under German management. As it was, external circum-

OAEG 2–8–0 No 107; these were the heaviest German engines in East Africa

25

*Hanomag 2–8–0 No 112 with a goods train loading firewood along the line about
forty miles east of Tabora*

stances made them one of the shortest-lived classes on the Central Line.

By 1912, it was decided to raise eventually the maximum permissible speed for the Tanganyika Express between Dar es Salaam and Kigoma to 60km/h and design specifications were prepared for new passenger locomotives. They were to be capable of hauling a 200-ton train on level line at 60km/h and on a 1 in 50 gradient at 15km/h. Twelve engines were considered necessary. No fewer than sixteen designs for four-, six- and eight-coupled engines were put forward by Borsig, Hano-

mag, Henschel and O & K in 1913–14, and of these, eight superheated 4–8–0s and four 4–6–0s were finally ordered in July 1914, but, as a result of the war, they were never supplied. The order was placed after much hesitation regarding the suitability of superheaters and feedwater heaters on wood-burning engines. Among the designs seriously considered but finally not accepted were a 2–8–2 proposal by Henschel, drawings of which were discovered at Tabora in the 1920s, and a Hanomag 4–8–2, which is shown below.

During the last days of German rule, the OAEG

Drawing 2A: Proposed 4–8–2 locomotive for the OAEG by Hanomag

possessed sixty-four locomotives, forty-four of them tanks and twenty tender and the general standard of the line and its equipment was quite high. Economic prospects were optimistically assessed, for European settlement and mining prospects were expected to contribute important revenue within the near future. Yet, the actual revenue of the Usambara Eisenbahn was considerably greater than that of the OAEG, mainly because of the fact that the latter's goal, Lake Tanganyika and thus the Katanga ores, were reached only just before the outbreak of the war, whereas the country itself was hardly developed to bring any revenue.

GERMAN EAST AFRICA 1893–1914

Wheel arrangement	Builders	Running numbers
	TANGA LINE	
0–4–2T	Vulcan Stettin, 1303–7, 1893	1–5
0–4–4–0T	Jung 414–18, 1900	1–5/6–10
2–8–0T	Orenstein & Koppel 2701–2, 1908	11–14
2–8–0	Orenstein & Koppel 4166–7, 1910	15–16
	5401–2, 1912	17–18
	CENTRAL LINE	
0–4–0T	Henschel 7063–4, 1905	1–2
	7485–6, 1905	3–4
0–4–0T	Markmaschinen 26, 1893	5
0–4–0T	Henschel 9528–31, 1909	6–9
0–4–4–0T	Henschel 7259–62, 1905	20–3
	8130 , 1907	24
2–4–4–0T	Henschel 9074–7, 1908	25–8
2–8–0T	Orenstein & Koppel 3223–6, 1909	41–4
2–8–0T	Borsig 7143–4, 1909	45–6
0–8–2T	Henschel 9301–2, 1909	47–8
2–8–0T	Borsig 7153–5, 1909	49–51
2–8–0T	Orenstein & Koppel 3312–14, 1909	52–4
2–8–0T	Borsig 7552–5, 1910	55–8
2–8–0T	Hanomag 5845–8, 1910	59–62
2–8–0T	Maffei 3628–31, 1910	63–6
2–8–0T	Hanomag 6589–603, 1911–12	101–15
	– 1913	116–20
	SIGI LINE (750mm gauge)	
0–6–0T	Orenstein & Koppel – , 1910	–

CHAPTER 3

THE UGANDA RAILWAY, 1895-1914

THE first members of the technical staff for the Uganda Railway stepped ashore in Mombasa on 11 December 1895. Chief engineer was Sir George Whitehouse, a man of considerable experience in railway building in three different continents. Work was started soon after and in May 1896 the first locomotives arrived together with twenty-five wagons, all bought from the Indian railways. Two of the engines were 2–4–0 tanks of class A, purchased secondhand from the Indian State Railways. Twenty-five of these engines were built in 1871–2 by Dübs of Glasgow, one of the constituent firms of the later North British Locomotive Company, as

works numbers 508–19 and 602–14. The second batch had greater fuel and water capacity than the first, but apart from this the engines were identical. These little engines had a long life; they were officially written off in 1903, but apparently this was by no means their definitive end, as one was reportedly sent to Tanganyika during the military campaign in 1917, where it was laid up during the same year. There were also two 0–4–2 tender locomotives of class E, besides six 2–6–0 tender engines of class N. Of this total of ten engines, the As were mainly used for shunting and line building purposes, being very light engines. The six Ns were

Dübs 2–4–0T class A, the first to serve on the Uganda Railway

28

E class 0–4–2, taken over from India together with the As

intended for main-line service; they were much in need of repair, but after overhaul gave reasonably satisfactory service. The Ns were built by Neilson in 1881 and 1884 in two batches of twenty and six respectively, as works numbers 2774–93 and 3445–50, for the Indian State Railways and the State of Mysore. The E class locomotives belonged to a series of twenty-two, built in 1878 by Dübs & Co as works numbers 1174–95 for the Indian State Railways. They were also very light engines of

just under sixteen tons service weight and were coupled to six-wheeled tenders carrying 80cu ft of fuel and 1,000 gallons of water. As in the case of the A class, the author has not discovered which engines were the ones for the UR.

Right at the outset it was decided to standardise the continuous air brake for the UR, as the line would reach altitudes, where the vacuum brake, although cheaper, was unlikely to give satisfactory results.

N class 2–6–0s being erected in the construction yard at Kilindini

While the second-hand engines were giving useful service as an interim measure, new engines were ordered from Britain. As the MacDonald Report had suggested in 1893, they were an improved version of the standard Indian F class, the UR locos also being class F. The first five, built by Messrs Kitsons of Leeds, went into service in 1896–7. They were 0–6–0 tender locomotives with outside frames and outside cylinders, while the valve gear was inside, and an unusual feature in the design was the fact that the big end of the connecting rods was inside the coupling rods. They had six-wheeled tenders for 2·3 tons of firewood and 1,500 gallons of water and, with a total weight of 48·8 tons, were substantially heavier than the N class. Built by Kitsons, Neilson and Vulcan, their total number rose to thirty-four in 1898. Later on, in 1911–12, three appear to have been sold to Messrs Pauling & Co for construction work on the line to the Lake Magadi soda deposits near the Tanganyika border.

During 1897 ten more N class 2–6–0s were obtained from India, followed by another four, bringing the total number of this type to twenty. They were lighter than the Fs, working at 140lb/sq in, developed 12,950lb tractive effort and were a useful help in the early days of the line. Three had Joy valve gear, the other ones Walschaerts motion. Having outside frames like the Fs, they could be recognised at a glance by the big Indian-type cowcatchers and flat-topped Belpaire firebox. They suffered from one serious defect in that they continually derailed on the hastily laid track; initially the track was not ballasted and probably

in a rather bad shape. Yet when, in 1897, a strike in the British engineering industry paralysed all locomotive supplies to East Africa, it was largely thanks to these locomotives that the construction of the UR continued.

During construction of the line, the conditions under which the engines worked were quite severe; temporary diversions with curves down to 400ft radius and gradients of 1 in 30 resulted in heavy wear on flanges and tyres, and the bad, often brackish, feedwater necessitated frequent boiler washouts. Many locomotive stations did not even have water taking facilities at all and had to be supplied with feedwater from elsewhere by tank train.

The N class engines soldiered on until well into the present century and the last ones were not withdrawn until 1931 by which time newer and far more powerful eight-coupled types were available. New engines of the B class were supplied by Baldwin of Philadelphia in 1900, thirty-six 2–6–0s with six-wheeled tenders. The order was placed in America because British manufacturers, after the strike of 1897–8, were choked with orders held over and consequently could not guarantee delivery within a reasonable time. The American engines were not considered to be finished in the same style as those built in Britain, but they were easier on the road, better suited for rough jobs during construction and generally did excellent work. They were unmistakably American in appearance with sandboxes on top of the boiler, conical boiler section, bar frames and outside cylinders with typically American slide valves in the shape of a

N and F class engines with construction trains at Athi River station

N class 2–6–0 engine; this class was the first to be introduced for main-line service

B class 2–6–0 No 62 with its crew. The American features of the class stand out by comparison with British designs for the UR

A B class 2–6–0 leaves the tunnel at Tunnel, near Kisumu

smaller box on the cylinder casing. Like the two previously built classes, the Bs worked all kinds of traffic and, especially during the earlier days of their career, were frequent on passenger trains. The American features which these locomotives introduced to the UR were not to be generally accepted for a long time to come. Bar frames, for example, came into use only in the late 1920s when the Baldwins had virtually disappeared from the scene.

These three classes suffered much during the initial days of the railway and by about 1910 were rather run-down. Before sufficient new engines could be obtained, however, war broke out and heavy military demands on the system, together with the non-availability of new locomotives meant that they were kept running, although they became very uneconomic. The last B and F class engines were finally retired between 1926 and 1930, the last three Bs from Kisumu shed in 1926. The last F worked at Nairobi workshops, where it had acquired an additional saddle tank between the chimney and the dome to give extra water capacity. It was scrapped in 1930.

Meanwhile, the railhead was advancing at a steady but unexpectedly slow pace. By the autumn of 1898, only a third of the expected mileage had actually been completed, mainly as a result of difficult terrain conditions and the engineering strike in Britain, which held up the delivery of already ordered locomotives. For the descent into the great Rift Valley, a temporary rope-worked incline with gradients of $9\frac{1}{2}$ to 50 per cent, overcoming a difference in altitude of 1,523 feet, was constructed, while the definitive alignment was being taken through an easier, though still tough, route. It was foreseen that the railhead would probably pass the Kikuyu Range before the permanent alignment could be ready and chief engineer Whitehouse decided to use the temporary construction to avoid unnecessary delay in track laying. The ropeway was opened in May 1900 and consisted of four sections, laid as double-track lines. As the advancing railway came from the highlands and proceeded into the Rift Valley, full wagons went down, their heavier weight being used to haul up empty wagons, speed being regulated by brakes on the cable drums at the top of the incline. On the middle portions the gradient was almost 50 per cent and here the wagons were taken on a kind of platform on wheels, running on 5ft 6in gauge with legs of uneven lengths to give a level top. The platform had a piece of normal track to carry a four-wheel

Carrier platform working on the ropeway down the eastern incline of the Rift Valley

wagon or a locomotive without its tender and the whole thing was also worked by steel-wire ropes passing round drums and attached to winding engines. The broad gauge for the carrier platforms was chosen to ensure lateral stability.

From the foot of the incline a temporary line was laid to the permanent alignment further on. After closure of the ropeway in 1901, the permanent alignment was changed twice, and the present third route came into use only in 1948. The alignment of the ropeway is still visible to the present day and was later used for power supply lines running down into the Rift Valley.

By 1910 the tonnage hauled had increased markedly and more engine power became imperative. Following a widely practised pattern of the time, the UR ordered two, followed by sixteen more, of the standard 0-6-6-0 compound Mallets from North British. These engines constituted the first attempt on the UR to get a comparatively high-powered engine for the light track combining it was hoped superior adhesive weight with the short coupled-wheelbase of the older six-coupled engines, to avoid flange troubles on the many tight curves. The new class, which featured the main air reservoir on top of the boiler, was in terms of tractive effort and sheer size a big stride forward in comparison to the earlier locomotives.

In service, however, these Mallets, supplied in 1913-14 and carrying numbers 101-18, proved something of a disappointment, for maintenance turned out to be unexpectedly heavy and failures in the joints of the low-pressure steampipes were frequent. No doubt lack of experience by maintenance staff had its effect but the Mallets quickly established a bad reputation. Modifications were incorporated in the second batch; the first two engines had been supplied with slide valves on all four cylinders, but the engines of the second and third batches had piston valves on the high-pressure side. As the engines worked with saturated steam all cylinders had outside admission.

In locally effected changes, the water capacity of the tenders was increased from 2,140 to 3,050 gallons and the compressors were repositioned from over the front power unit to a position alongside the firebox, within the driver's reach to enable him to use a hammer in case of failure, which were all too frequent. After the war, the Mombasa-based Mallets were arranged to burn oil fuel, as the shed at Kilindini was equipped with oil-refuelling facilities. Oil burning equipment became general practice for all Kilindini-based locomotives during the 1920s.

Problems with uneven running remained, because of the big low-pressure cylinders of $24\frac{1}{2}$in $\times$ 20in, the absence of a leading pony truck, insufficient adhesive weight on the power units and the

33

C

MT class 0–6–6–0 with increased tender capacity and non-standard number plate

small diameter driving wheels of only 3ft 3in, which severely limited maximum speeds. Moreover these engines were used on heavy goods trains, which were often on tight schedules of lighter trains. As a result they quickly became run down. These tribulations certainly shortened their life and in the late 1920s when the newly acquired Garratts had proved successful, all the Mallets were scrapped. The last two in service were KUR 105–6, working from Nairobi shed until about 1930. After this experiment and with the clearly superior performance of the Garratts the KUR never returned to the Mallet concept.

At about the same time as the Mallets arrived new tank engines were ordered. The only tanks available at the time were the old A class, barely capable of doing anything more than light shunting work. Three side-tank 2–6–2 locomotives were built in 1913 by Nasmyth Wilson & Co for shunting and light branch-line work, becoming class S, and later, in 1929, class ED. For branch duties they carried additional fuel and water supplies in an auxiliary tender behind the engine, for the bunker capacity was only $1\frac{1}{2}$ tons of coal, or 75 cubic feet of firewood, and 800 gallons of water. They were, however, mainly used for shunting

ED class 2–6–2T shunting engine

work in the Mombasa harbour area and, like many Kilindini-based engines, were converted to burn oil fuel about 1920. All these early oil burners used the British system with the burners inbuilt at the back of the firebox under the firehole door, compared to the American system now in use, where the burners inject oil backwards from the firebox front end.

The successful operation of the S class engines resulted in an order for a slightly modified tank locomotive, also supplied by Nasmyth Wilson as a 2–6–4T, eight of which were supplied in 1913–14. Known as MS class, changed in 1929, when the engines became class EE, they were mainly identical with the 2–6–2Ts, but had increased fuel and water capacities. Notwithstanding this improved capacity, they, too, needed auxiliary tenders

when working branch trains, as on the Nairobi-Nanyuki and, later, Kisumu-Butere lines. An additional reason for the use of these tenders was the rapid loss of adhesive weight and consequent slipping when water from the side tanks was used. In branch-line work, the EEs managed 150 tons, or eight of the old four-wheel coaches, at 30mph, despite driving wheels of only 3ft 7in.

The EE class was due for replacement by 1939, but was kept in service during World War II and they only disappeared in the middle 1960s by which time they had been renumbered EAR 1001–8. One, EAR 1003/KUR 393/UR 93/63, has been preserved and stands, beautifully restored in its original graphite livery, in Nairobi's Jamhuri Park as UR 63. This engine was built by Nasmyth Wilson, works No 1011 in 1913.

An EE class 2–6–4T (as EAR No 1004) stands at Kisumu station with a passenger train for Butere. Note the auxiliary tender

STEAM LOCOMOTIVES OF EAST AFRICAN RAILWAYS

UGANDA RAILWAY, 1895–1914

Class	Wheel arrange-ment	Builders	Running numbers
A	2–4–0T	Dübs & Co (508–19, 602–14) 1871–2	
E	0–4–2	Dübs & Co (1174–95) 1878	
N	2–6–0	Neilson (2774–93, 1881) (3445–50, 1884)	
F	0–6–0	Kitson 2362–6, 1896 Neilson 5288–93 } 1897 5349–51 } Vulcan 1594–605, 1897	
B	2–6–0	Baldwin 16969–74 } 17032–9 } 1899–1900 – }	50–79 –
MT	0–6–6–0	North British 19648–9, 1912 19989–94, 1913 20272–81, 1914	101–18
S (ED)	2–6–2T	Nasmyth Wilson L 980–2, 1913	81–3
MS (EE)	2–6–4T	Nasmyth Wilson L 1009–13 } 1913 L 1041–3 }	61–8/91–8/ 391–8

CHAPTER 4

THE FIRST WORLD WAR, 1914-1918

THE outbreak of World War I in August 1914 put the UR in a difficult position; the main line ran for a considerable distance parallel to the frontier and only a short distance away. For this reason all locomotives initially were concentrated at a few points, those on the line between Kisumu and Nakuru at Nakuru, and those between Mombasa and Nairobi at Nairobi. Thus, all traffic came to a standstill, but later when it resumed, the situation was complicated by the cessation of freight from the German ports on Lake Victoria, which had contributed about 20 per cent to the total volume on the UR.

Despite the strained situation, expansion of the locomotive stock continued, and three 2–6–4 EE class tanks and seven 4–8–0s were put in service. The 4–8–0s were the first locomotives in East Africa with this wheel arrangement, of which eventually many more were to follow. They were modelled upon locomotives built in 1905 for the Assam Bengal Railway in India and were initially classified G, later GA and finally, in 1929, EB. Built by Nasmyth Wilson, they were often referred to as 'ABR-type locos'. They represented a welcome addition to the stock of overworked N, F and B engines and were a straightforward and useful design; as the first eight-coupled types they shared the heavy traffic, in those years at the modest level of barely sixty million ton-miles, with the then new Mallets.

A Kilindini-based GA was the first locomotive on the UR to be converted to oil fuel, which had been under consideration since 1899, but never introduced to any extent. Until about 1900 coal was used as fuel, imported initially from India and later from Wales. After then, as the railway reached the wooded highlands, a change to wood fuel was made to reduce expensive and cumbersome coal imports.

During the war, locomotive losses on the UR were happily few, but one EE tank engine was driven into a river by a German raiding party, and some B and N engines were mined. The strain on the railway was greatly increased when in 1916 a full-scale military invasion into German territory was launched. To ease operations, a supply line

UR G class 4–8–0 locomotive, later reclassified EB

OAEG 2–8–0 No 108, deliberately run down a blown-up bridge by the German army during the military campaign

was built from Voi to Maktau, which was eventually extended to Moshi on the Tanga-Arusha line on German territory, the first goal of the offensive. Thus, the two systems were physically joined and supplies ran through to the south, although this proved difficult as the German system used vacuum brakes compared with air brakes on the UR. One of the few positive results of the war was the accelerated introduction of electric light on the locomotives, after initial experiments with searchlights on an armoured train unit in use for line patrols.

German East Africa was the only German colony in Africa not relatively easily overrun by the allied forces early in the war, and it was not until 1916 that a successful invasion was undertaken, after an abortive attempt in 1914. Even after this invasion it took until the end of the war to gain control over all German territory.

The German railways were as heavily committed as the Uganda line and military transport formed the majority of traffic worked. When the military situation grew worse much of the permanent way, bridges and culverts were destroyed and locomotives driven into the ruins to form huge piles of

wreckage, intended to impede the British advance. Consequently, when the British occupied the northern part of German East Africa, they brought their own locomotives with them; like the earliest UR types, they had been imported from India.

These Indian exiles totalling twenty-five engines, belonged to four different classes with 0–6–0, 2–6–0 and 4–8–0 wheel arrangements. Ten were later put to work on the Central Line and fifteen on the Tanga Line. Besides these British-built engines, many German locomotives were later salvaged and restored to service although in the longer term they did not find much favour, apparently because of certain German locomotive design features that differed substantially from British practice. For example, the ratio of heating surface of the boiler tubes to that of the firebox was substantially higher in the German case and this led to proportionally higher stresses on the firebox and thus, inevitably, to higher maintenance costs.

Of the imported engines on the Central Line, five were standard 4–8–0 tender locomotives belonging to class G (for goods) of the Assam-Bengal Railway, the same engines on which the design of the UR GA class was based. They had

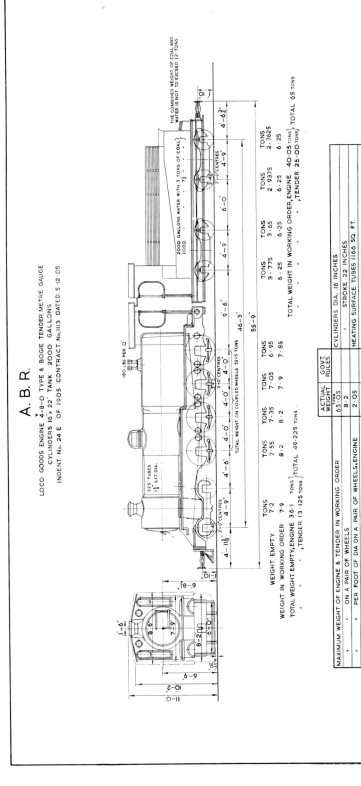

A. B. R.

LOCO GOODS ENGINE 4-8-0 TYPE & BOGIE TENDER METRE GAUGE
CYLINDERS 16" x 22" TANK 2000 GALLONS
INDENT No. 24 E OF 1905 CONTRACT No.1113 DATED 5·12·05

	ACTUAL WEIGHT (TONS)	GOVT. RULES
MAXIMUM WEIGHT OF ENGINE & TENDER IN WORKING ORDER	65·05	
" " ON A PAIR OF WHEELS	8·2	
" " PER FOOT OF DIA ON A PAIR OF WHEELS, ENGINE	2·05	
" " " " " " " " ,TENDER	2·63	
" " " " WHEEL BASE, ENGINE	1·884	
" " " " " " ,TENDER	1·612	
" " FOR ENGINE & TENDER TOGETHER PER FOOT RUN OVER BUFFER	1·166	
WEIGHT ON COUPLED WHEELS	32·15	

CYLINDERS DIA. 16 INCHES
STROKE 22 INCHES
HEATING SURFACE TUBES 1166 SQ. FT.
FIREBOX 126 " "
TOTAL 1292 " "
FIREGRATE AREA 17·5 " "
TRACTIVE FORCE TAKING 90% OF BOILER PRESSURE 2l2l8 Lbs.
" " 75% " 17652 "
RATIO OF TRACTIVE FORCE TO ADHESION = 90% = 3·39
" " " " " " = 75% = 4·07

DIAGRAM OF ENGINE & TENDER

Drawing 3: ABR G-class 4-8-0 locomotive

C.M.E's DRG. No. E.A.R. (MECH.) O9388

TRACED FROM MESSRS RENDEL & ROBERTSONS DRG. No. 495/2

SCALE ONE QUARTER INCH TO A FOOT

been designed by the British Engineering Standards Association (BESA) and built by North British in 1905 in a batch of ten, NBL numbers 17305–14. The five newest were lent to the British Expeditionary Force in East Africa in November 1915 and arrived in Africa early in 1916. The engines still carried the legend 'Assam Bengal Railway' and their original running numbers 125–9. They belonged to a standard type of locomotive and were in use for six years, until 1922 when they were returned to India.

Then there were four similar 4–8–0s built by Nasmyth Wilson in 1915 for the Nizam's Guaranteed State Railway (NGSR). To assist in the invasion of German East Africa they were commandeered in March 1916 on their way to India and diverted to East Africa, where they were impressed in service, still carrying their original numbers NGSR 1095–8. In contrast to the ABR engines, these Nizams never reached their original destination, but spent their entire working life in Tanganyika, where they were scrapped during the 1950s. More details on their later life are given in chapter six.

These two 4–8–0 classes set the pattern for new Tanganyika locomotives for a considerable time to follow and the 4–8–0 wheel arrangement in the course of time became widely used. Engines of this type were built by the hundred over many years for widely separated countries throughout the African continent. East Africa alone (UR plus TR) was to receive a total of 128 4–8–0s until 1930, in several progressive developments of the same basic type, those remaining now forming EAR classes 22, 23 and 24.

The tenth engine on the Central Line belonged to the old 0–6–0 Indian F class, of which there were twelve on the Tanga Line, together with three 2–6–0 M (for Mogul) class engines. The Fs had been built by mainly Dübs, Neilson, Vulcan and, later, North British from 1874 onwards, and they originated on the Burma Railway (BR), Bombay, Baroda & Central India Railway (BB&CI) and the Madras & Southern Mahratta Railway (MSM), in numbers of three, four and five respectively.

The ex-BB&CI engines belonged to a batch of twenty-one built in 1894 by Dübs & Co as works numbers 3133–53. The M class 2–6–0s came from the ABR where they carried the numbers 61, 62 and 67; they were Hanomag-built in 1901. Finally, there were two locomotives that had been obtained from the UR, a B class 2–6–0, No 35, and a 2–4–0 tank of unspecified type, but presumably one of the two very first UR locos of the once-Indian A class. If this engine, about which no further details are known, really was one of the by then quite old As (they dated back to the early 1870s), it may not come as a surprise to know that it was soon taken out of service and laid up.

Apart from these locomotives, there appear to have been a number of classes in use with the Expeditionary Force, but there is some confusion here, as in several cases engines that clearly belong to the same class are mentioned in records with different class letters. Besides the locomotives that eventually came to the TR, there were in any case five Q class 4–8–0s, reportedly built by North British in 1904 to the Indian standard 4–8–0 design, to which both G classes also belonged, and eleven B/SB 4–6–0s, at least seven of which were supplied, also by North British, in 1906–7 to the Bengal & North Western Railway. These locomotives never came to belong to either the UR or the later TR, however, on loan or otherwise; immediately after the war the locomotives were returned to India and are therefore not treated in detail here.

After the war while the reconstruction of wartime damage started, the area which until then had been known as Deutsch-Ostafrika was taken over by Great Britain under a League of Nations mandate, and renamed Tanganyika.

LOCOMOTIVES IMPORTED IN TANGANYIKA DURING WORLD WAR I

Class	Wheel arrangement	Builders	Running numbers
F	0–6–0	Vulcan	81, 83, 96 (BR)
		Dübs & Co (3133–53)	73, 111, 127, 186–7
		Neilson	(MSM)
		North British	649, 695, 719–20
			(BB & CI)
G	4–8–0	North British 17310–14, 1905	125–9 (ABR)
	4–8–0	Nasmyth Wilson L 1050–3, 1915	1095–8 (NGSR)
M	2–6–0	Hanomag 3814–15, 3822 , 1901	61–2, 67 (ABR)
A	2–4–0T	Dübs & Co, 1872	(UR)
B	2–6–0	Baldwin, 1899–1900	(UR)
B	4–6–0	North British, 1906–7	
SB	4–6–0		
Q	4–8–0	North British, 1904	

CHAPTER 5

THE UGANDA/KENYA-UGANDA RAILWAY, 1919-1940

AFTER the war, when traffic on the UR returned to normal conditions, a start was made to replace worn-out locomotives in the shortest possible time. Many of the older types were in a run-down condition even before the war and the heavy demands during hostilities had only made things worse, especially in the case of the old six-coupled types. The GA class 4–8–0s were considered a good basic type with which to continue and, in 1918, UR ordered thirty-four more of these Indian-inspired engines from North British. Being some five years newer they were classified GB. Just like the GAs, they were built for saturated steam, working at the relatively low pressure of 160lb/ sq in. With about 20,000lb tractive effort and 8–9

tons axle loading, they performed satisfactorily in mixed traffic, so much so even, that the last ones, by then reclassified initially EB1 and finally EAR 2218–23, were not withdrawn until 1964. Four EB1s, Nos 2220–3, together with two of the later 24 class, were used during the construction of the Western Uganda extension, the last important part added to the EAR network in the 1950s. Until 1954 the locomotives on the extension were based at Kampala and then transferred to Musosi, which thus became the first 22 base on the extension proper. They still served as wood burners in 1955 and were retired when, in 1955–6, oil fuel instal-lations were erected.

Many of the EB1s were sold as scrap to Japan,

KUR class EB1 4–8–0 No 161

EB2 class 4–8–0, the first superheated design for the UR

from where several parts of their equipment had to be repurchased later on. It was said that even the copper fireboxes alone were worth more than the £90 apiece the engines brought in as revenue!

Yet, the good results of the GB/EB1 notwithstanding, the UR did not want to close its eyes to new developments and, in the same year that the first GBs were supplied, 1919, two superheated 4–8–0s were ordered from Messrs Nasmyth Wilson & Co. These engines, too, were very similar in general arrangement to the older ones, but were equipped with piston valves in conjunction with a

Robinson superheater of rather modest dimensions, providing only 167 sq ft heating surface. These were delivered in 1921 and initially classified GC, later changed to EB2. They were used in extensive trials to investigate the value of superheating, which they proved beyond any doubt. The two EB2s were still very much Indian-looking engines, with a sunshade cab on the tender to provide a protected resting place for the crew during stabling periods. The main reservoir for the Westinghouse brake was positioned on top of the boiler in the same fashion as the Mallets. The two EB2s were written

EAR 2423 of the former EB3 4–8–0 class at Nairobi shed in December 1972

off in 1934, having been heavily worked as trial engines, but superheating had been proved and, with the sole exception of the ED1 shunters, all further UR locomotives were superheated.

During the early 1920s increased European settlement in the Kenya Highlands brought a rapid traffic increase and in 1923 total ton-miles had gone up to over 120 million. To handle this volume a larger and modernised version of the EB2 was ordered as class GD, later EB3 and today known as EAR class 24. Their performance was a big step forward and they were the first locomotives to be built in any substantial numbers for East Africa with piston valves and superheaters. The EB3 design, supplied by Vulcan and Nasmyth Wilson between 1923 and 1930, hardly ever got the credit it deserves as one of the most successful locomotive types ever produced in East Africa. Mail trains, through goods, stabling duties, engineering trains, in all these jobs the EB3 could and to the present day still can, be found. In fact they accept every train, on whatever traffic they are used, and still they are the mainstay of traffic on lightly laid lines, with their axle load of only ten tons. According to present plans, thirty-five will be kept as reserve power after dieselisation and as such they will thus survive all other steam power, including the post-war classes 29, 30 and 31, built 1951–5!

The first thirty-eight EB3s, Nos 162–99, were supplied with the same 17×22in cylinders as the EB2 and with tenders for 2,500gal water. Later batches incorporated modifications: from No 200 (EAR 2439) onwards, cylinder diameter was increased to 18in and the tenders replaced by a slightly larger version for 3,500 gallons. Both tender versions are still in use at present, although not necessarily coupled to the original engines, the small ones being preferred for duties on shorter branch lines. All cylinders were later standardised at a diameter of 18in.

Originally, the first engines were built for partly mixed wood and coal burning and partly for coal only, but fifteen working from Kilindini shed in Mombasa, were equipped to burn oil, following earlier trials with other classes. The oil-burning engines were built by Vulcan in 1923 and had running numbers 167–81. Like another early oil-burning class, the 2–8–2 EAs, the EB3s reverted to coal in the early 1930s and worked as a mixed wood- and coal-burning class until after World War II, when the EAR as part of its policy to free itself from coal imports from South Africa, adapted all its main-line engines to burn oil fuel. The last pre-war oil-burning EB3 was No 174.

Coal, imported from South Africa had been reintroduced as locomotive fuel in 1926, when the newly acquired Garratts had shown poor results on wood fuel. In the old days, mixed wood- and coal-burning engines had a crew of four, one driver and three firemen or an apprentice driver and two firemen, who relieved each other in firing. The photograph on page 31 shows Baldwin engine No 62 with its crew as an example. The EB3, however, managed with a crew of three. Firewood, or *kuni*, was normally thrown rather carelessly on the tender at intermediate stops en route and this practice fairly often led to logs being lost on sharp curves. Consequently, men working along the line were extra cautious when an engine passed to avoid being in the way of a falling log.

The UR had reached Kisumu on the shore of Lake Victoria, then called Port Florence, in 1901 and traffic to and from Uganda went by rail to Kisumu and from there onwards by lake steamer. This situation continued until the 1920s, when the railway was extended to Uganda proper by a new line that branched off at Nakuru and ran via Eldoret and Tororo to Kampala, reached in 1931. During this time, in February 1926, the railway changed officially to its new name of Kenya-Uganda Railway (KUR).

This new line conquers one of the more difficult railway stretches in the world, climbing to an altitude of 9136 feet, the highest point reached by a railway anywhere in the Commonwealth, on the Uasin Gishu Plateau. It was laid with 50lb rail, allowing a maximum axle loading of ten tons. The EB3s were obviously no match for the challenges this new line presented, especially in the case of heavy traffic. In fact, these locomotives were already facing troubles with heavier trains on the sections west of Nairobi and it was clear that some more effective type had to be thought of. One possible solution was the Mallet, but after the discouraging experiences with the MT class 0–6–6–0s the KUR was, understandably, not over-enthusiastic to risk another misfortune. It was thus decided to try another articulated type, the Beyer Garratt, which had shown to give satisfactory results in other countries where comparable conditions prevailed, as for instance in South Africa.

The basic Garratt consists of two power bogies, each with its own cylinders, between which a strong girder frame, carrying boiler, firebox and cab, rests on two pivots, while fuel and water supplies are carried directly on the power bogies. The first Garratts were built before World War I and were quite modest engines, but by the middle

EC class 4–8–2 + 2–8–4 No 41, the first Garratt class for the KUR

1920s the type had evolved into sizeable locomotives with a respectable amount of power. One
of its main attractions was that it permitted fairly
free development of the boiler and firebox, without
restrictions imposed by the fact that they had to
be carried on a single frame. Its advantages on lines
with tight curvature are obvious. The four Garratts of class EC that Beyer Peacocks supplied to
the KUR in 1926, numbers 41–4, were basically
two of the standard EB3s put back to back together
where motion and wheel arrangement were concerned, with an additional pony wheel at the inner
end of each power bogie. The cylinders were
smaller than the EB3's, but wheel diameter and
drive on the second coupled axle were retained,
the cylinders being steeply inclined in the same

fashion as on the 4–8–0s, to reduce vertical forces
at the crossheads with the short driving rods. Axle
loading was limited to ten tons, enabling the
engines to work on 50lb track. With these locomotives, the KUR introduced the 4–8–2 + 2–8–4
wheel arrangement that was to become so widely
used all over the world. The ECs were equipped
with the flat-topped Belpaire firebox which had
been favoured by the UR for many years.

Initially, the Garratts were tried on the normal
Eucalyptus wood fuel, but this was found to be
impracticable. On the Nairobi-Nakuru line firing
was extremely heavy and wood consumption high,
the fuel 'going straight out of the chimney' as one
driver put it; and extra wood-carrying wagons were
required to give sufficient fuel supply. After this

EAR No 1110 of the former ED1 2–6–2T class at Nairobi shed

abortive experiment the ECs were converted to burn coal and these engines were in fact one of the main reasons for the at least partial return to coal firing. The four ECs proved useful in heavy mixed traffic and were the forerunners of many more Garratts to come, indeed they were the turning point in the KUR policy as far as heavy loco-motives were concerned. Until the end of its sepa-rate existence, the KUR ordered only two more classes of conventional locomotive, both at about the same time as the Garratts.

First was the ED1 class 2–6–2T, of which twenty-seven were supplied from 1926 to 1930. In most respects they were similar to the earlier EEs, but reverted to the original wheel arrangement of the ED class. With a slightly higher adhesive weight than the EE class, they were in service on branch-line traffic, but mainly as shunters, and as such they are at work to this day, renumbered EAR 1105–31. The ED1s were the last KUR design to be built for saturated steam and with slide valves. The second non-articulated class was the EA,

originally conceived in the middle 1920s as a 2–8–2T class for heavy shunting duties in the Mombasa harbour area. For this purpose the har-bour track was relaid in 80lb rail, the engines being designed with a high axleload of 17–18 tons. Eventually another design was evolved for this purpose as an 0–6–0T of the proposed class EG, which then failed to materialise. Drawings of this proposed tank engine exist, showing a shunter of about 43 tons service weight.

The EAs, as built by Messrs R. Stephenson in 1928, were 2–8–2 tender locomotives of quite im-pressive appearance with big, high-pitched boilers, 4ft 3in driving wheels and big bogie tenders. All six carried names of local origin besides their numbers, the first KUR locomotives to do so. The engines were built from the outset to burn oil fuel and they had an interesting career, in fact they might be regarded as a classic example of the merits of regular drivers, what in French is called the *machine titulaire* system. In their early days, these locomotives were indeed driven by regular

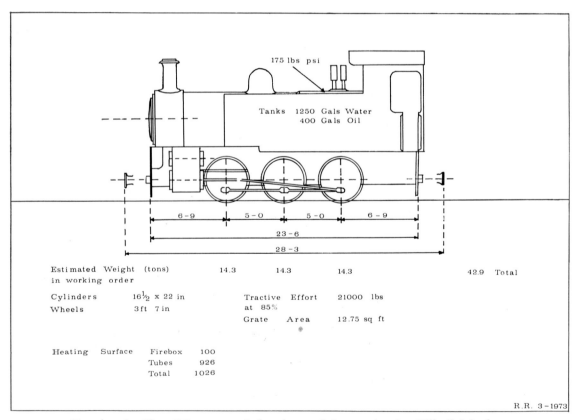

Drawing 4: Class EG, proposed shunting tank locomotive for Kilindini harbour

EA class 2–8–2 No 4 Kilifi *in later days as EAR 2804*

crews and although initially they were not allowed to operate on main-line services, mainly as a result of their 17·5 tons axle loading, they never gave any trouble.

The latter fact made the KUR reassess their duties and the EAs were put on the mail trains between Mombasa and Nairobi, although at first confined to the line section Mombasa-Makindu. From 1932, however, when 80lb track reached Nairobi, they were allowed to run the whole distance. From Nairobi onwards the mail trains were then taken over by a Garratt for the difficult section to Nakuru on 50lb track. To ensure regular drivers, two drivers were allocated to one engine and this was the start of caboose working. Drivers' names were painted on inside the cab roof. Ten round trips per month between Nairobi and Mombasa were regular, a total distance of 6,600 miles, while a long month meant $10\frac{1}{2}$ trips. In this way all EAs completed over a million miles by 1950.

The heaviest non-articulated locomotives on the metre gauge in the Commonwealth, the six EAs, numbers 1–6, did splendidly as long as they were handled by drivers with sufficient technical knowledge. Indeed they needed 'personal' attention, especially for the standard type of white-metalled axleboxes, in conjunction with high axle loadings. A special cooling system, working with water from the tender, was fitted to prevent axleboxes running hot.

In 1929, to bring the EA class more in line with the other engines they were converted to burn coal and equipped with manually-operated rocking grates. They steamed so freely on coal that they were dubbed the 'firemen's friends', but a problem was their rather rough riding, probably due to their big cylinders and high centre of gravity on the one hand, and insufficient balance in the reciprocating masses on the other. Although equipped with compensated spring gear throughout, they bounced and leaped quite violently when running at speed, sometimes causing the crew to seek refuge on the tender!

When the EAs were pooled they almost immediately started giving trouble with hot axle-boxes, despite the cooling system. In 1948, when the EAR introduced oil burning on all main-line locomotives to free itself of coal imports, the class reverted to oil burning. At the same time, holes were drilled in the crescent-shaped balance weights to reduce the balanced percentage from two thirds to forty per cent to improve riding. This measure is difficult to understand and was not satisfactory, for the riding qualities decidedly deteriorated. For the re-conversion to oil firing the engines were fitted with American-type oil tanks with a capacity of 2,375 gallons as against 3,000 gallons for the original tanks with which Stephensons had supplied them. Other changes were the introduction of power reversing gear and Timken roller bearings, which finally solved the axlebox problem. Thus receiving a new lease of life, the EAs, renumbered EAR 2801–6, were used on heavy freight trains and their maximum permissible speed was raised for

Two EC1 4–8–2+2–8–4s in EAR days working an up goods train at Timboroa summit

the generally tighter schedules. They had not been designed for this type of work, however, and unsatisfactory running, together with several cases of broken side rods and frame bars, led to them being taken out of service and stored. This proved to be the beginning of their end; several times they were reintroduced to traffic and then put into store again, but finally they were taken out of service and scrapped. To the present day, older drivers still regard them as the best engines the KUR ever had, claiming that their lives would have been much longer had they been kept in the hands of their regular drivers instead of being pooled, and had they been kept on fast passenger services for which they were originally built.

To return to the 1920s, the results of the EC

Garratts were such that in 1928 twenty more were delivered, generally similar but with increased coal and water supplies and, as a consequence, slightly heavier. They were classified EC1 and numbered 45–64. These engines, too, gave excellent service and were in service until the middle 1950s but for two, sold together with the original four ECs in 1939 to the Yunnan railway in French Indo-China, making room for newer and heavier Garratts. No 45 was originally supplied with a Weir pump and feedwater heater, following the practice of certain Tanganyika locomotives of the period of classes MK and RV. The results obtained, however, were not considered of sufficient importance and the equipment was removed.

Two further EC1s were built in 1930, numbers

Engine No 66 EC1, one of the two experimental EC1s built in 1930

65–6, but they differed in several respects from the earlier ones. They were a more or less experimental development with slightly different tanks and, of more importance, a much wider blastpipe and chimney than had been used on the earlier EC1s, to diminish back pressure more effectively. Three superimposed conical petticoats were used to ensure sufficient boiler draught. They had arch tubes in the firebox and in this altered form did indeed steam more freely than the standard version, but for some reason this idea was not adopted as standard. Moreover, No 66 had the French ACFI feedwater heater on the boiler, as yet another experiment to improve the thermal efficiency of the locomotives. This device gave maintenance trouble because of its complexity and was later taken off, again without having given decisive advantages. When in 1948 the EAR renumbered all locomotives these two EC1s were classified separately as 5101–2, whereas the standard EC1 became class 50 (5001–18). All the Garratts, in their early days, were driven by regular crews and not just any driver was allowed to handle them. No doubt this system has contributed considerably to their outstanding service record and the high mileages between overhauls.

In 1931, a third Garratt type was introduced as class EC2, later EAR 5201–10. This class was exceptionally built by North British instead of Beyer Peacock, the engine showing minor differences by comparison with the EC and EC1 classes to avoid infringement of Beyer Peacock's established patents. After the expiry of the original Garratt patent in the 1920s the design became open to other manufacturers as well, although Beyer Peacock normally kept a lead by having constructional refinements registered as separate patents. Apparently, this was not without its value, for the EC2 class, although reasonably successful, was the only Garratt class for the KUR not built by Beyer Peacock, and in fact it was NBL's only Garratt design. It was mainly modelled on the EC1 class 4–8–2 + 2–8–4, but incorporated some of the novelties of the two non-standard locomotives 65–6, including the arch tubes in the firebox; they also had a rearranged water capacity. Their tractive effort was slightly higher than that of the EC1. All EC2s were fitted with mechanical lubricators to feed the coupled axleboxes at the crown. The class remained in service until the late 1960s, by which time they had migrated to the Central Line in Tanzania, and when they were finally taken out

Class EC2 4–8–2 + 2–8–4 No 73 at Nairobi

D

Class EC3 4–8–4+4–8–4 No 80, one of the most successful Garratt classes of the KUR

of service, No 5210 (North British 24079, 1931) was preserved for museum purposes.

In 1939, the KUR introduced yet another type of Garratt locomotive, the 4–8–4+4–8–4 EC3 class, six of which were supplied initially, followed by two more in 1940 and four in 1941. These engines revolutionised working on 50lb track, developing 47,200lb tractive effort with an axle loading as low as $11\frac{3}{4}$ tons, the maximum permissible on this light track. Numbered 77–88 and later EAR 5701–12, they had a boiler diameter of 6ft $6\frac{1}{4}$in or almost double the track gauge, working at 220lb/sq in and the total weight went up to $186\frac{1}{4}$ tons, of which 94 was adhesive. They were exclusively coal fired.

Besides its wheel arrangement the EC3 embodied many other design novelties; for the first time on a KUR Garratt, bar frames and a round-top firebox with thermic syphons had been incorporated in the design, and the driving wheel diameter of 4ft 6in represented a substantial increase over the 3ft 7in of the earlier Garratts and even over the 4ft 3in of the EA class 2–8–2s. They were fitted with roller bearings on the carrying wheels and had hard grease on the coupled axle-boxes and soft grease on the motion. Self-cleaning smokeboxes, chime whistles, air-operated firehole doors and cylinders drain cocks, and steam rocking grates were provided.

The leading set of coupled wheels on both power bogies was flangeless to ease clearances on tight curves. Also, the practice of rather steeply inclined cylinders, a heritage of the 4–8–0s necessitated by the fact that the drive was on the second coupled axle, was discontinued and cylinders were placed horizontally. Drive was therefore shifted to the third coupled axle, to minimise vertical forces at the crosshead, a practice retained by Beyer Pea-

cock in all subsequent Garratts. The crossheads themselves moved in double overhead slidebars, an arrangement that has always been kept as standard on KUR/EAR engines.

Like all subsequent locomotives on the system, the EC3s were designed with easy conversion to 3ft 6in gauge in mind, through simple changing of wheel tyres. The wheel has a broad rim, upon which the tyre is shrunk. Converting the engine to 3ft 6in gauge is accomplished by moving the tyres outward on the rim to the new gauge and adjusting the brake equipment accordingly. In practice, the idea of conversion to Cape gauge (3ft 6in), although conceived as long ago as 1928, has been impeded by shortage of funds ever since, and in the mid 1960s expenditure was estimated at roughly £20 million, which effectively prohibited implementation. Eventually, regauging would be accompanied by a change to the MCB coupler which is, however, being contemplated by the EAR anyway.

The practice of naming which had been introduced in 1928 on the EA class, was continued on the EC3 locomotives, which received names of areas and localities along the Kenya-Uganda main line, and was continued after World War II on other classes as well, also on conventional locomotives. After some teething troubles the EC3s proved to be a highly successful design, working the heaviest traffic during the war under difficult circumstances and reaching average mileages of more than 200,000 between heavy repairs.

Liberalisation of the permissible loading gauge on the KUR in the years after the war permitted the raising of the very flat boiler mountings and the fitting of steam collectors under the raised domes. This was intended to reduce priming by providing an extra dry steam space, but the measure had no effect at all and priming continued as before. In one case of unofficial modification, that of engine 5705, even an extra preheater was built in under the dome, but like the pre-war experiments on EC1 Garratts it did not lead to any important improvement in boiler efficiency and was as quickly taken off again.

In their original form the EC3s had one live steam and one exhaust steam injector, but after about ten years of service both were replaced by two normal Monitor injectors. The engines were also supplied with thermic syphons, but they were not successful and indeed could cause trouble, for at the summit of steep gradients the water level, which had been sufficient against the gradient, could suddenly drop and expose the crown sheet. All EC3s at some time or another blew a lead plug and as a result of this the thermic syphons were removed.

Today, only one EC3, No 5711 and formerly KUR 87 *Karamoja,* is left and this engine is being kept for the EAR railway museum, for which purpose it will be brought back to its original condition, without the Giesl ejector fitted in 1962, and in the graphite livery of the former KUR. This particular locomotive was built by Beyer Peacock in 1940 as works number 6974.

Class EC3 4–8–4+4–8–4 as EAR No 5708 Gulu, in the intermediate condition with raised boiler mountings, runs into Nairobi yard with a freight train from Mombasa

STEAM LOCOMOTIVES OF EAST AFRICAN RAILWAYS

UGANDA/KENYA-UGANDA RAILWAY, 1919-1940

Class	Wheel arrangement	Builders	Running numbers
G (GA, EB)	4–8–0	Nasmyth Wilson L 1034–40, 1914	121–7
GB (EB1)	4–8–0	NBL 22527–60, 1919	128–61
GC (EB2)	4–8–0	Nasmyth Wilson L 1350–1, 1921	119–20
GD (EB3)	4–8–0	Vulcan 3556–60 ⎱ 1923	162–6
		3578–92 ⎰	167–81
		3788–805, 1925	182–99
		3863–80, 1925–6	200–17
		Nasmyth Wilson L 1580–5, 1930	218–23
ED1	2–6–2T	Vulcan 3886–91 ⎱	
		3917–31 ⎰ 1926–7	10–32 ⎱ later Nos 310–36
		4079–80 ⎰	
		Bagnall 2377, 1929	33
		Hunslet 1655–6, 1671, 1929	34–6
EA	2–8–2	Stephenson 3921–6, 1928	1–6
EC	4–8–2+2–8–4	Beyer Peacock 6300–03, 1926	41–4
EC1	4–8–2+2–8–4	Beyer Peacock 6429–40 ⎱ 1927	45–64
		6516–23 ⎰	
		6637– 8, 1930	65–6
EC2	4–8–2+2–8–4	NBL 24070–9, 1931	67–76
EC3	4–8–4+4–8–4	Beyer Peacock 6905–10, 1939	77–88
		6970–75, 1940	

CHAPTER 6

THE TANGANYIKA RAILWAY, 1919-1940

UNDER British administration the Tanganyika Railway started operation on 1 April 1919. It took over a collection of locomotives of mainly German origin, together with the engines brought in by the British forces during the war. Circumstances were certainly difficult in the beginning; the retreating German army had thoroughly demolished the entire railway and it took a considerable time before all damage had been repaired and acceptance of traffic meanwhile was very severely restricted.

On several points the repairs needed on the

Central Line meant the virtual building of a new line and this was used as an opportunity to realign some of the tightest curves, an activity which resulted in a shortening of the distance between Dar es Salaam and Kigoma by about four miles.

Of the German locomotives, four classes were initially put into service on the Central Line, 14 of the Hanomag-built 2–8–0 tender locomotives of the former class 101–20 and now classified GG for German Goods, 22 2–8–0Ts, the German *Einheits-vlok*, now called class GT, for German Tank, 2

GT class 2–8–0T shunter at Tanga; two of these engines were the last
German locomotives in TR service

53

0–8–2 tanks and 6 0–4–0T pugs, dating back to the earliest years of the line, when the DKEBBG had used them for line building purposes. Later on, a total of seven 0–4–4–0T and 2–4–4–0T Mallets were also reconditioned.

On the Tanga Line only five German locomotives were put in service again, three of the Orenstein & Koppel-built 2–8–0 tender locomotives of the German series 15–18 and two of the standard 2–8–0 tanks. Many of the Hanomag engines on the Central Line needed new cylinder castings, as the Germans had destroyed them in an attempt to prevent subsequent use of the engines. The new castings were made at the Parel works in Bombay of the former Great Indian Peninsula Railway and mostly fitted at Tabora, where the Germans had installed the main workshops for the Central Line. Thus 14 engines could be reconditioned, Nos 102–3, 105–6, 108, 111–17, 119–20.

At first optimistic estimates were given for the useful life of the tender locomotives, but later in service they proved something of a disappointment to the British railwaymen; one of the reasons was probably that they were built to different construction principles rather than being badly built engines. Whatever their qualities, the two 2–8–0 tender classes disappeared after a fairly short life in comparison to other, British-built locomotives on the system. The first engines went in the early 1920s, when money was made available to buy new engines from Britain. The remaining Hanomag locomotives were laid up in about 1932, after the arrival of the new class GA Garratts. One, however, was temporarily brought back into service in 1937, equipped with an electric headlamp, to work the engineering train on the lightly laid Mwanza line, which was very susceptible to washaways, and was always troublesome to operate from the locomotive point of view. All the Mallet tanks were derelict at Tabora works in 1930–1 and were subsequently sold as scrap to Japan. Only the 2–8–0T engines had reasonably successful careers under British auspices, both on the Central and the Tanga Line. Although degraded to shunting duties during the 1920s, two continued on the Tanga Line until after World War II; these last two relics of German times finally worked in the Tanga harbour area, where they showed an unattractive tendency to run away on the steep grade to the port, ending up in the fish market, to the mutual damage of both. Their water tanks eventually took on a distinctly armoured appearance through frequent repairs. Both engines, Nos 101–2, were finally scrapped at Nairobi works in

1951. They originally belonged to the Orenstein & Koppel batch of 1908, but the author has been unable to determine which two engines of this batch of four were the survivors.

Of the imported British-built engines, the thirteen ex-Indian F class locomotives were already aged by the time they reached East Africa in 1916. The bulk of them had been built during the 1880s and 1890s and they originated on different railway systems on the Indian subcontinent. One went to the Central Line and twelve to the Tanga Line. Of these, the largest batch of five came from the MSM and these were numbered 73, 111, 127, 186–7. They had, at least partially, been built by Vulcan, whose works number for No 73, 1739 of 1899 is the only one the author has been able to trace with certainty.

Three Fs came from the BR, Nos 81, 83 and 96 and four from the BB&CI, Nos 649, 695, 719–20. The oldest F locomotives are said to have been built in 1874. Most returned to India in 1922, but two Fs, Nos BR 96 and BB&CI 720, remained in service on the Tanga Line, where they worked the mail trains as a double-headed pair until the arrival of new 4–8–0s of class G in 1928. The general manager had complained earlier about the high maintenance cost and the considerable trouble that had been taken to keep these two obsolete locomotives running. Consequently, No 720 was scrapped in 1928 but No 96 was transferred to the Central Line, where it remained in service, working inspection trains, until 1937, when it too was finally retired.

The British-built 4–8–0s have been described in some detail in chapter four; originally, they were built for the ABR and NGSR, respectively. Both classes were practically similar in dimensions to the UR G class, the later EB, which was derived from the ABR engines. They went back to India in 1922. The closely similar NGSR engines were put in service with the lettering NGSR and the numbers 1095–8. This was changed to TR 1095–8 and as such the locomotives were in service for many years. Finally, in the early 1930s, they were reclassified NZ, for Nizam, and renumbered 200–03. In their early days, they suffered a good deal from stresses, as the Central Line had initially been relaid to much of the original first German formation, which incorporated extremely tight curves. On the sharpest curves the rails had to be greased by gangs of workmen to allow the engines to pass. Yet the Nizams had a long and distinguished career, remaining in service until after the amalgamation in 1948, when they became EAR 2201–4

TR class NZ 4–8–0 No 1098 leaving Dar es Salaam with the mail train in 1922

In the late 1940s, two were transferred to the newly constructed Southern Province Railway, built in connection with the ill-fated groundnuts scheme. Nos 2202 and 2204 were scrapped in 1952, and 2201 and 2203 in 1956, after 40 years' service.

The last class of ex-Indian locomotives consisted of three 2–6–0s of class M (for Mogul) built by Hanomag in 1901 for the ABR. They were numbered 61–2 and 67. Their design was not superlatively modern and they were suitable only for lighter mixed traffic, in which duties they served until 1922, when they were returned together with most of the war-imported engines. They had Hanomag works numbers 3814–15 and 3822.

Traffic had gradually increased beyond the capacities of the four Nizams and the salvaged German engines, and new locomotives became an imperative need in the early 1920s. The first to be built for the TR were six 4–8–0 tender locomotives of class DL, supplied by Beyer Peacock in 1923.

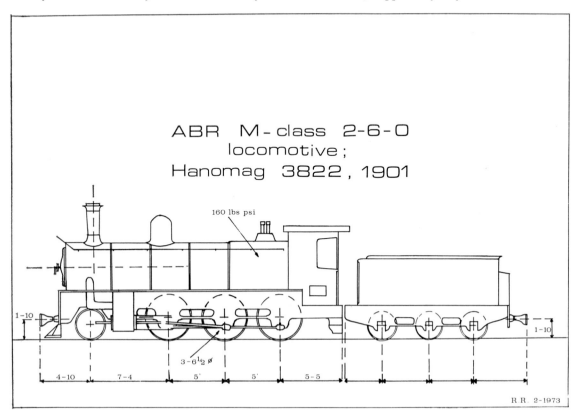

Drawing 5: M class 2–6–0 locomotive

DL class 4–8–0 as EAR 2306 on shunting duties at Nairobi

The abbreviation DL stood for Development Loan, after the funds that had been made available to finance the rehabilitation of the line and its further improvement. These locomotives, running numbers 200–5 and later 300–5, showed no Indian characteristics and were in fact a more modern design, having piston valves and superheaters in contrast to the slide valves and saturated steam of the Nizams. They were derived from the lighter engines of the Nigerian Railways' Emir class. Like them they had narrow fireboxes which were found to be less suitable for wood burning, so that the DLs were used mainly on the section between Dar es Salaam and Morogoro, where coal was available. Attempts were also made to use them on coal on the section from Morogoro to Dodoma, but the experiments were not too successful and often ended up with a badly clinkered fire long before Dodoma was reached. Nevertheless, the DL was a useful type and the engines are still in service as EAR class 2301–6, having migrated in recent years to Tororo in Uganda, but their days are numbered and 1973 was expected to be their last year in service, after a useful life of 50 years.

Ex MK class 2–8–2 EAR 2508, arrives at Mwanza station with the mail train from Tabora

To remedy the shortcomings of the DL's narrow firebox it was clear that an engine with a deep and wide firebox would be needed, to allow for both coal and wood fuel. To this end an engine was designed with a 2-8-2 wheel arrangement and a bigger boiler than that of the DL with the required type of firebox. Locomotives of this type were supplied by Vulcan in 1925–6 as class MK, short for Mikado, a designation which has been in general use since the first locomotives of this type were built for Japanese railways by American firms. Some years later it was discovered that the Germans had planned a remarkably similar 2-8-2 in 1912, apparently in an attempt to overcome the same sort of problem. Probably their 2-8-0s of the series 101–20 had similar problems to the DL, having similar fireboxes.

The MK was a great success and to the present day these engines are valued by the crews; as class 2501–11 they are still in service on the Central Line, although their time is now running out as well. One problem in the design of the MK was the fact that the leading pony truck provided insufficient guidance on the sharp curves on the Dar es Salaam-Morogoro and Malagarasi-Kigoma sections, and the design of the Bissel truck left something to be desired. This was presumably seen as a

general shortcoming of locomotives with a leading pony truck and the obvious solution was thus to redesign the engine as a 4-8-2. Of the latter type, eight were supplied by Vulcan in 1928–30 as class RV, short for River; the engines were named after major rivers in the Territory and numbered 250–7, later changed to 500–7.

The basic MK 2-8-2 was a generally satisfactory design and no alterations were made beyond what was absolutely necessary to adapt it as a 4-8-2; only the frames were extended 2ft 9in to accommodate the leading bogie. As a result of this change it was found necessary to extend the smokebox to keep the cylinders at least roughly in line with the blastpipe and chimney. The same boiler of the MK class had been retained for standardisation purposes.

Here, however, lay the root of the weaknesses of the RVs; for the greater length of the smokebox created vacuum problems, resulting in insufficient boiler draught. In consequence the RVs were poor steamers and this manifested itself clearly in their early days when they worked the mail trains on the Central Line. They were particularly bad on the Dar es Salaam-Morogoro and Kigoma-Kazuramimba sections with ruling gradients of two per cent and more, although the below-average

RV class 4-8-2, EAR 2102 Ruvuma, *at Morogoro in July 1972*
57

EAR 4–8–0 No 2214 leaving Mtwara with the first official train on the Southern Province Railway in 1954

quality of firewood on the western section also had something to do with these poor performances. The RV class quickly established a bad reputation for itself with the crews, even more so as the introduction of a leading bogie had spoilt the weight distribution, despite a much-improved ability to negotiate curves. Although this was later corrected to a certain extent, their adhesive weight originally was slightly less than that of the 2–8–2s, a feature that was to reappear in 1955 when the 2–8–2 29 class was redesigned as a 2–8–4.

Both MK and RV were equipped from the outset with Weir feedwater heaters, the first on the TR. They were positioned on the left running board alongside the smokebox and it was this device, supplying the boiler with a steady flow of hot feedwater instead of intermittent cold water from injectors, that helped the RVs to work on difficult sections without serious fall in boiler pressure. The preheaters have been retained to the present day, and clearly found favour in Tanganyika, yet the KUR, despite several experiments, did not find them advantageous. As EAR class 2101–8 the RV class locomotives were at the time of writing working out their lives on lighter duties from Morogoro shed but were unlikely to survive beyond 1973.

The four Nizam 4–8–0s obtained in 1916 served as the prototype for the TR's own G class, a very similar unsuperheated, slide-valve engine, thirteen of which were supplied by Stephenson and Nasmyth Wilson and put in service in 1928–31. They were again closely similar to the original BESA-designed 4–8–0s for India and thus provide, as the last 4–8–0s built for the TR, a direct link with the first engines of this wheel arrangement to see service in this part of the world. The first eight were supplied to the Tanga Line in 1928 and released F class engines 96 and 720, which had become very expensive to maintain. One of the new Gs, unassisted, could handle the mail trains, a marked improvement over the old and obsolete six-coupled engines. The G had an axle load of only 8–8½ tons, a necessity on the light track of the Tanga Line. The reason for their obsolete concept is not quite clear, however, if we remember that these engines were built at the same time as the KUR EA class Mikados. Their original running numbers 20–32 were later changed to 204–16, as the locomotives were considered to be direct descendants of the NZ class locomotives 200–3. After the amalgamation in 1948 the G class engines were renumbered 2205–17 and gradually taken out of service; at the time of writing only one, 2215 at Morogoro, remains in service. This engine is scheduled to be kept for the railway museum. It was built by Nasmyth Wilson in 1930 as No L 1589.

Renumbering scheme of TR locomotives

Class	Old number	New number	EAR number
NZ	1095– 8	200– 3	2201– 4
G	20–32	204–16	2205–17
DL	200– 5	300– 5	2301– 6
MK	206–16	400–10	2501–11
RV	250– 7	500– 7	2101– 8
ML*	700– 5	600– 5	2601– 6
GA	300– 2	700– 2	5301– 2
ST	11–14	103– 6	1101– 4
GSL	1– 8	51– 8	—

* The ML class was supplied in 1947 with the numbers 700–5; on receipt, this was changed to 600–5, as the 700 series of numbers was in use for the GA class Garratts.

As described in preceding paragraphs, the TR changed all running numbers in the early 1930s to a much more logical and consistent system than that used by the KUR. Each class started at a round figure in series blocks of hundreds, a much easier system to understand than the continuous numbering of the KUR, where many engines received numbers that happened to be free, as in the case of the EA class Nos 1–6, or were simply numbered in order of arrival, as was the practice in the early days of the UR.

During the 1920s, the Tanganyika Railway system was enlarged by the construction of two new lines, an extension of the Tanga Line from Moshi to Arusha, planned in German times, and the planned scheme from Tabora to Ruanda-Urundi modified to terminate at Mwanza on

Sentinel GSL class shunter No 57 at Tabora

GA class 4–8–2+2–8–4 Garratt No 302 heads the Dar es Salaam-Kigoma mail train

Lake Victoria. Ruanda-Urundi, formerly German territory but under Belgian mandate at this time, was no longer considered relevant.

The Moshi-Arusha extension was laid with 45lb rail, to allow use of all TR locomotives then in service. The original plan of the German colonial administration to extend the line south of Mount Kilimanjaro to the lake was altered to one calling for a line from Moshi to the Central Line, but this idea was not pursued either.

In 1930 Vulcan supplied to the TR four 2–6–2T shunters of the same type as the KUR ED1 class, which became class ST, running numbers 11–14 and later 103–6. The sole difference from the KUR ED1 was the latter's Westinghouse brake equipment and compressor. After the amalgamation the engines were incorporated in the EAR 11 class, together with the ED1s, and became Nos 1101–4. Many of the 11s, adapted to burn oil fuel, are still in use today on various shunting duties.

For lighter shunting work at smaller stations eight geared four-wheel Sentinel locomotives of class GSL were supplied in 1929–31. These engines formed an interesting and successful experiment. Among their duties in the following two decades they were used as shed pilots, particularly for hauling out larger engines from the German-pattern roundhouse sheds to the turntable, an arrangement frequently used at Central Line depots. After the war, they began showing signs of age and as newly built steam shunters were not readily available, they were replaced by diesels, the first on the TR. The last Sentinels, although outmoded, served at Tabora until the middle 1950s before being scrapped.

For the most difficult parts of the Central Line three 4–8–2+2–8–4 Beyer Garratts were ordered from Beyer Peacocks just before the depression. The order was placed after several years of successful Garratt operation on the Kenya-Uganda system and the locomotives were based upon the KUR EC2 class, but had narrower front tanks and consequently a reduced water capacity to suit permissible axle loadings on war-damaged bridges on the Central Line. Originally these class GA Garratts carried numbers 300–2, but later they were renumbered 700–2. With an axle load of 10–10½ tons and 46,200lbs tractive effort they proved of utmost operative advantage even during the depression, when traffic volumes declined greatly. Operating costs were markedly reduced after their introduction and during World War II years they proved to be indispensable. It was therefore unfortunate that one of them, No 702 *Bukoba*, plunged into a washaway near Mikese during a night of bad weather in 1944; although the crew fortunately were saved, the engine was almost completely submerged and had to be written off.

The two survivors were taken over by the EAR as 5301–2. Like several other Garratt classes, the GAs were named, in this case after the places where the TR had its big road depots, *Arusha* and *Iringa;* the third engine *Bukoba* carried this name as there was a jetty for marine services in that town. Following the example of the last KUR EC1, No 66, they were also equipped with the French-inspired ACFI feedwater heater. Partly as a result of the same maintenance troubles experienced by the KUR and also because of only limited improvement in thermal efficiency they were later discarded.

In EAR days the two 53s went to the northern part of the now united system, to be replaced on the Central Line by the newer 60 class, but later they returned to Tanzania, for transfer work in Dar es Salaam, where they were scrapped in the late 1960s. The only other Garratt type on the TR was class GB consisting of four 4–8–2+2–8–4 engines brought from Burma after the war and numbered 750–3, later EAR 5503–6; they are described in more detail in chapter seven.

Apart from the two Garratt classes, the TR standardised on the orthodox eight-coupled rigid design with variations. This policy was made possible by the generally easier profile of the Central Line compared with the KUR main line, but, surprisingly, introduction of such 'real' express passenger types as the 4–6–0 or 4–6–2 was never considered. There was one exception, however, in the case of the four 4–6–0s of class

BB, introduced second-hand in 1947; they were not successful and were never used on main-line duties. More details are given in chapter seven.

The 750mm line Tengeni-Sigi in Tanganyika, mentioned in chapter two, closed in 1924. Following protracted disputes between the Usambara Planters' Association and the Tanganyika Government, the Sigi line was planned for reopening in 1929. The line was to be reconditioned and a new locomotive ordered from Messrs Hudson & Son of Leeds, who sub contracted to Kerr Stewart in 1930. It was a geared 0–6–0 industrial engine with a Willans multi-tubular boiler and was introduced more or less as an experiment, after satisfactory results with comparable locomotives in Natal. Unfortunately the Sigi line locomotive turned out to be a complete failure. The boiler feed mechanism was unsatisfactory, but as the builders, Kerr Stewart, meanwhile had been liquidated, there was no chance to have modifications carried out to correct the faults as was suggested by experts during an enquiry in 1930. Moreover, by 1930, the economic situation caused by the depression had changed drastically since reopening had been agreed in 1928 and the planned rehabilitation of the line was abandoned, as hopes of an adequate return on the necessary investment looked dim indeed. As for the locomotive, its end was as sad as that of the line itself; after the enquiry in 1930, it was found totally unsuitable for use and while still virtually new, was scrapped.

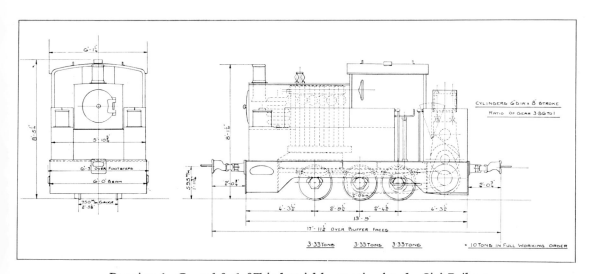

Drawing 6: Geared 0–6–0T industrial locomotive for the Sigi Railway

STEAM LOCOMOTIVES OF EAST AFRICAN RAILWAYS

TANGANYIKA RAILWAY 1919–1940

Class	Wheel arrangement	Builders	Running numbers
		For ex-German and war-imported locomotives see pages 27/41	
NZ	4–8–0	Nasmyth Wilson L 1050–3, 1915	1095–8/200–3
DL	4–8–0	Beyer Peacock 6128–33, 1923	200–5/300–5
G	4–8–0	Stephenson 3959–63 } 1927	20–32/204–16
		Nasmyth Wilson L 1588–91, 1930	
MK	2–8–2	Vulcan 3892–6, 1925 3942–7, 1926	206–16/400–10
RV	4–8–2	Vulcan 4318–20, 4352–3, 4426, 4447–8, 1928–30	250–7/500–7
GSL	0–4–0T	Sentinel 1929–31	1–8/51–8
ST	2–6–2T	Vulcan 4490–3, 1930	11–14/103–6
GA	4–8–2+2–8–4	Beyer Peacock 6718–20, 1930	300–2/700–2

CHAPTER 7

THE SECOND WORLD WAR AND ITS AFTERMATH, 1940-1949

WORLD War II broke out on 3 September 1939 and immediately East Africa, and with it the railway, was brought to a war footing. Military transport, safety precautions, all these troubles again showed their ugly heads, although one comparative advantage existed compared with 1914 for Tanganyika was not enemy territory this time. Ethiopia until 1941 was in Italian hands, but this never really threatened the KUR, and the TR even less, although the Italians initially launched an offensive against Kenya and indeed partly occupied its northern area. A new element, largely unknown in World War I, was air raid precautions, introduced some time after the war broke out resulting in black-out measures that severely hampered normal working.

When war broke out the KUR was in the process of taking delivery of its new 4–8–4+4–8–4 EC3 Garratts. They were received between 1939 and early 1941, just in time to give a much-needed uplift to the available motive power. Older engines like the 2–6–4 EE class were due for replacement by that time, but in the circumstances they had to be kept in service during the period of hostilities and even much longer, the EEs not being scrapped until the 1960s.

Military transport requirements strained the railway to the utmost and both staff and equipment had very little rest. The new EC3s ran in this abnormal situation more than 200,000 miles between heavy repairs, far more than had been allowed before the war, without giving any serious

KUR class EC4 4–8–2+2–8–4 EAR No 5402 the last in service, with the down mail at Limuru station

trouble; one engine even reached the figure of 243,000 miles.

Nevertheless, new engines were badly needed and it was with great relief that the KUR received seven new powerful Garratts of class EC4 in 1944. The EC4s, later EAR 5401–7, were again 4–8–2+2–8–4s and with fourteen tons axle load were limited to main-line work on 80lb track. They had been designed to War Department requirements and wartime conditions were responsible for the fact that they were not satisfactory. Although they had a most useful tractive effort of some 58,000lb, the non-availability of heavy steel for bar frames and their consequent construction with plate frames, meant that they were structurally weaker than desirable. The plate frames combined with the small 3ft 9in wheel diameter and the general rush to complete them brought complaints and problems for crews and maintenance staff. The engines could hardly manage the heavy trains for which their high tractive effort had predestined them, as they always tended to tear themselves to pieces.

Beyer Peacock originally built the same basic design in two versions a 2–8–2+2–8–2 for 3ft 6in gauge, in which form it served in several African countries and, modified for the KUR metre gauge as a 4–8–2+2–8–4 to carry more water, higher axle loadings being allowed than in most of the other countries concerned. After the war the EAR drew up plans to convert the 54s to the same 2–8–2+2–8–2 wheel arrangement as the 3ft 6in gauge locomotives, but this plan never materialised and it is hard to see how this change would have improved them in any substantial way.

Besides their known existing weaknesses, the operating authorities made the same mistake with these locomotives as that with the UR Mallets long before—they were put on faster schedules than those for which they were best suited; as a result they often returned from such duties to shed with many components having worked loose. The photograph on page 63 shows No 5402, the last in service, with a down mail train in Limuru station; it was this sort of working which ultimately at least was partially responsible for the 54s' bad reputation where maintenance was concerned.

Working from Nakuru shed in the early 1960s, they were stored shortly afterwards, reintroduced for a short time and transferred to Mombasa and there finally scrapped. The last survivor No 5402, worked heavy traffic in the Mombasa harbour area. In retrospect, they were by far the shortest-lived Garratts in East Africa, all except one having been scrapped by the mid 1960s, after only about twenty years' service.

Directly after the war, when it became clear how much both systems had been overworked, the KUR and TR strove to obtain new locomotives. Nominally financial results had been very good, but it was much more a paper profit than a real one. As railways all over the world were mostly in comparable circumstances, new locomotives ordered directly after the war could not be supplied by the manufacturers without considerable delays, as many builders still had pre-war orders to fulfil. Waiting periods of five to six years were not uncommon and consequently many railways had to be content with second-hand locomotives as a stop-gap measure to meet their most urgent requirements.

Several standard locomotive types had been evolved in various countries during the war years for this sort of problem, to serve on both standard and narrow gauge in different countries after the war. In this category, the American 'MacArthur' 2–8–2 wartime austerity locomotives are well known and they saw service in geographically widely separated areas all over the world including, later, Tanganyika.

Both KUR and TR were lucky to obtain a batch of another wartime 4–8–2+2–8–4 Garratt design, respectively classified EC5 and GB. They had a complicated history, for they were originally designed for Brazil in 1939, but not actually built because of the outbreak of the war. During hostilities, when the War Department needed a suitably light but powerful engine for use in the Far East, this design was brought out from its file and twenty locomotives were built in 1944–5 for India and Burma. Two, however, went straight to the KUR as class EC5 Nos 120–1 in 1945, while the TR bought four others in 1946 from Burma, where the political upheavals of the period prevented their intensive use, and made them class GB, running numbers 750–3. In 1949 both classes were integrated into one class, becoming EAR 5501–6. Like the EC4, they had round-top fireboxes and plate frames but were much lighter and therefore trouble free and more successful than the heavy EC4/54 class. Five more, EAR 5507–11, were bought from Burma in 1952, having been BR class GD; rehabilitation of the Burmese network was still hampered by terrorist activities and in consequence these engines had seen only limited service.

In the immediate post-war years the 55 class

One of the 4–8–2+2–8–4 Garratts bought by EAR from Burma, No 5509, seen at Nairobi shed in 1972 as fitted with Giesl ejector and chimney

Garratt No 122 EC6, shortly before being renumbered EAR 5601, leaves Nairobi on its first trial run

E

*Garratt 4-8-4 +4-8-4 No 5810, fitted with Giesl ejector and chimney, ready to leave
Nairobi with an up goods train for Nakuru in May 1972*

was a very welcome addition to the locomotive stock and proved to be highly useful. Today, equipped with Giesl ejectors, a number of locomotives are still hard at work, mainly from Voi to the Tanzanian part of the system, although scrapping has now begun. The 55 design was so successful, in fact, that it served as a prototype for several progressive locomotive developments in and outside East Africa. The first of these classes, supplied by Beyer Peacock at the time of the merger of KUR and TR, received KUR designation EC6 and numbers 122–7, although already supplied with the lettering EAR on the tanks, thus making an interesting, though temporary, blend of old and new on the line. In contrast to the 55s, the EC6 (EAR 56) engines had Belpaire fireboxes in the old KUR tradition, and roller bearings on the bogie axles. Shortly afterwards they were renumbered 5601–6. The 56s had also been built for Burma as class GE in 1949, but the continuing trouble in that country meant that these six went straight to East Africa, while four others ended up on the Indian metre gauge. These engines were the first to feature the streamlined fuel and water tanks which after the

war became standard Beyer Peacock practice. They are generally considered as the best Garratts ever to see service on the EAR.

Another type to be perpetuated was the 4-8-4+4-8-4 EC3, and eighteen further engines of this type were supplied by Beyer Peacock in 1949–50. The only differences from the pre-war version were ½in greater cylinder diameter, while the liberalisation of the loading gauge permitted the boiler mountings to be higher. Initially, these engines had piston tail rods, a rather un-British feature, but they were removed in later years. Like the earlier EC3s, they had roller bearings on the bogie axles only. Ordered directly after the war as KUR 89–106, they should have received EAR numbers 5713–30, but the authorities decided to classify them separately. When the first EC3s arrived, the EC4s which already carried numbers 89–95 were renumbered 100–6, but before the whole EC3 class had been delivered the new numbering scheme had come into force and all engines were renumbered in September-October 1949, and the balance of class EC3 entered service as 5808–18.

Like the 57s, the 58 class gave excellent service

and at the time of writing scrapping has only just begun, the first engines being retired after more than twenty years of hard slogging work on the old KUR main line where they spent their entire life. In recent years, since the demise of the 57 class, advantage has been taken of the interchangeability of the boilers of the two classes and some 58s have received 57 boilers and even cylinders; the latter boilers are easily recognised by the flat-topped domes.

Boiler troubles are now in fact one of the main reasons for the withdrawal of the 58s. Indeed the class is somewhat underboilered and in consequence and because of the round-top fireboxes, suffered more than the other Garratt classes from priming. Priming results from the water surface lifting when the rate of steam release becomes too great and water is carried into the steam pipes. Dirty feedwater, forming a scum on the fiercely boiling surface, aggravates this tendency, which is an ever-present risk in heavy and continuous operation of steam locomotives on steep gradients. The danger of priming is reduced by the use of the flat-topped firebox of the Belpaire type, which is beneficial in that the area of water surface is increased in relation to the round-top firebox, as is the steam space above. Although the manufacture of the Belpaire firebox is more difficult and expensive, subsequent maintenance costs are lower than in the case of the round-top type. This reasoning is behind the fact that almost all East African engines, with few exceptions, were fitted with a flat-topped firebox until the very end of steam power development.

The end of the war found the TR in similar trouble to the KUR; traffic had increased enormously and the locomotives had received less attention and done more work than in normal times. A second point of some importance was the ill-fated groundnuts scheme, initiated in the immediate post-war years to meet a worldwide shortage of edible oils and fats. Of this scheme, which was to cover some three million acres in Kenya, Tanganyika and Northern Rhodesia (now Zambia), eighty per cent of reserved areas were located in Tanganyika. This is not the place to go into detail on this scheme, which finally turned out to be an abysmal failure, but in the late 1940s it put a heavy strain on the railway's capabilities.

To ease traffic, six new 2–8–2 engines of an improved MK class were supplied in 1947 by Messrs W. Bagnall as class ML, Nos 600–5. More were needed, but there was no chance to obtain them in under three years; six further engines of

this type were ordered as well as two prototype 2–6–2T shunting locomotives as an improvement on the existing ST class, for delivery in 1951. For its immediate needs, however, the railway had to be content with equipment that could be taken over and a widespread search for suitable second-hand metre-gauge locomotives was initiated. Four suitable 4–8–2+2–8–4 Garratts were traced in Burma; they were almost new and belonged to the light WD type. These locomotives, BR class GD, were bought from the War Office and arrived in Dar es Salaam in 1946. Numbered 750–3 later EAR 5503–6, they immediately went into service, giving good results on the heavier sections of the Central Line.

A second type acquired consisted of four 4–6–0 tender locomotives found at El Shatt, at the southern end of the Suez Canal opposite Suez. These engines were originally built in 1926 at Ajmer works in India for the BB&CI Railway and during the war nine were taken to Egypt to serve on the metre gauge Qena-Port Safaga railway from the upper Nile to the Red Sea. The 4–6–0s were found lying idle at El Shatt in 1945 and four were initially taken over by the TR in 1947–8.

They were not successful in Tanganyika, in fact they were considered poor engines; the round-top fireboxes gave trouble and non-standard parts had been used in their construction. Hence, the five remaining engines were not taken over, while the four that had come to the TR as class BB (for BB&CI), Nos 270–3 later EAR 2001–4, were used mainly for shunting and occasional banking duties. They led a somewhat shadowy existence and even a good photograph of them does not seem to exist, the only one known showing No 272 with its old TR number being cut up at Dar es Salaam about 1957–8.

The third second-hand type obtained by the TR was the American-built 2–8–2 MacArthur austerity locomotive. These engines were built by the hundred by such major US manufacturers as Alco, Baldwin and Davenport for use on narrow-gauge systems where no serviceable locomotives were available. Although possessing its share of shortcomings as an austerity, the MacArthur did much good work in many countries until long after the war. The CME of the TR, Mr W. Bulman, was able to purchase eight cheaply from the Malayan Railways in 1949 and put them in service as class MR, running numbers 800–7. The engines in question had been built by the three manufacturers mentioned, and though all were supposed to be of the same type, there were minor

Engines of the BB 4–6–0 class being dismantled at Dar es Salaam about 1958

TR 2–8–2 No 802 of the MacArthur austerity class at Tabora in the early 1950s,
before the conversion to oil fuel

differences between those of different builders. With an axle load of nine tons and 4ft driving wheels the MacArthurs were intended for a wide variety of duties on lightly laid lines, to form a sort of universal locomotive. At first there were problems, and modifications were needed to water tanks and reversing gear, which was undertaken at Nairobi works because of the limited capacity of the shops at Dar es Salaam. An additional difficulty was posed by the fact that the engines had not been designed to burn wood fuel. Grates were rather small and no rocking or dropping equipment was available. This circumstance gave rise to criticism because of the high ash residue of the wood fuel and only after the locomotives were converted to burn oil was the problem satisfactorily solved. After conversion the MacArthurs by then classified EAR 2701–8, did reasonably

well, although they did not come up to the level of the 25 class. Yet they had their good points, for instance their mechanical lubricators which were generally praised.

In 1950 eight more were purchased from Malaya and becoming numbers 2709–16, and one more was obtained in parts from Nigeria and erected at Dar es Salaam in 1953, becoming No 2717. The whole class was in service on the Central Line until the middle 1960s, when the boilers, to an ever increasing extent, began to cause trouble. Thus withdrawal became necessary and they gradually disappeared. The last one in service, No 2711, based at Tabora, had been kept running by cannibalising other members of the class.

The last new locomotives for TR had partly been supplied at the time of the amalgamation in

Tanganyika Railway class SS 2–6–2T delivered in 1950 as EAR No 1202 in its altered form with Giesl ejector shunting at Tabora

69

1948 and the balance was delivered to the EAR. These were the second batch of the ML class 2–8–2s and two SS class 2–6–2T shunters, which became EAR 2607–12 and 1201–2, respectively. The 12 class engines were the first superheated piston-valve shunters in East Africa; they are a generally updated and modernised version of the 11 class. Both engines were put to work in the harbour area in Dar es Salaam, from where they were transferred to Morogoro in the mid 1950s and eventually to Tabora in the early 1960s, where they are still in service. The 12 class are the only shunters with Giesl ejectors.

Much knowledge had been gained about the MK class engines since their introduction in 1925 and the improvements they needed, which were incorporated in the design of the ML 2–8–2s. Cylinders and valve gear were carefully modified, superheaters enlarged, roller bearings were fitted and a bigger tender than that on the MK (25) class was provided. The Weir pump and feedwater preheater were retained as they had given good results on both MK and RV classes. The new locomotives were mainly intended for service on the flatter sections of the Central Line between Dodoma and Tabora. They are still in service, although at present relegated to secondary duties, but their service record proved less favourable than that of the older 25s. They are definitely heavier on maintenance and their active life will probably end shortly, together with the 25 class, when both are replaced by new diesel locomotives.

In 1948, Kenya-Uganda Railways & Harbours merged with Tanganyika Railways & Port Services, after several years of preparatory discussions, to form East African Railways & Harbours, from which the 'Harbours' component was again dissolved in 1969. All locomotives and rolling stock were taken over by the new administration and from September 1949, all engines were renumbered, except two old ex-German 2–8–0 tanks of class GT about to be scrapped, and the Sentinel shunters in the same position. A numbering system was introduced whereby the class number forms the first two digits of the total and the engine's running number the last two. The first engine of class 26 thus became 2601, the eleventh of class 58 becomes 5811, etc. Tanganyika had used a comparable system of running numbers, but still used letters for the class designation, although even then the system was easier and simpler that that of the KUR. Under the new system, tank engines were allotted class numbers 10–19, tender engines 20–49 and Garratts 50 upwards. Diesels, then still only on order, were to become 80 upwards. Similar locomotives in service on both systems were taken together in one class, as was the case with the ED1 (KUR) and ST (TR) classes, both becoming class 11, nos 1105–31 and 1101–4 respectively. In some cases, engines that belonged to one class were given separate classifications, as was the case with the last two KUR EC1s, which became class 51 as against 50 for all others.

Once again, possibilities of standardisation with the railways in Rhodesia and South Africa were explored with the resulting consequences of regauging, introduction of MCB couplers and standardisation of brake equipment. This latter would have been a retrogressive step for the united EAR system, which had standardised on Westinghouse air brakes, compared with vacuum equipment in the other countries.

KENYA-UGANDA/TANGANYIKA RAILWAY, 1940–1949

Class	Wheel arrangement	Builders	Running numbers
		Kenya-Uganda Railway	
EC3	4–8–4+4–8–4	Beyer Peacock 7290–307, 1949	89–95 (96–106) EAR 5808–18
EC4	4–8–2+2–8–4	Beyer Peacock 7075–81, 1944	89–95/100–6
EC5	4–8–2+2–8–4	Beyer Peacock 7158–9, 1945	120–1
FC6	4–8–2+2–8–4	Beyer Peacock 7280–5, 1949	122–7
		Tanganyika Railway	
GB	4–8–2+2–8–4	Beyer Peacock 7150–1, 7157, 7146, 1945	750–3
BB	4–6–0	Ajmer Workshops BB & CI Rly, 1926	270–3
ML	2–8–2	Bagnall 2832–7, 1947	700–5/600–5
MR	2–8–2	Alco (nos 800–2) ⎫ Baldwin (nos 803–5) ⎬ 1944 Davenport (nos 806–7) ⎭	800–7

CHAPTER 8

EAST AFRICAN RAILWAYS, 1949-1973

THE newly established EAR inherited an over-worked locomotive stock and an impressive backlog of goods to be transported, especially from Mombasa harbour to destinations upcountry. The situation was complicated by the relatively rapid recovery after the war and the resulting traffic boom. New locomotives were thus a dire need and the new administration made this high priority. Some engines were already in hand; the KUR had ordered the 13 class 0–8–0 tank engines from North British as series 1301–18, a class which in fact materialised as a 4–8–2T to improve its running, and which carried more fuel and water. Then there were the 58 class Garratts in course of delivery. Sixteen heavy 2–8–2 tender locomotives, modelled on a class in service on the

Nigerian Railways were also on order as 2901–16. For the TR two 2–6–2Ts of class SS and six additional 2–8–2 MLs were on order, while nine further MacArthur austerity 2–8–2s were obtained from Malaya and Nigeria.

Clearly, this was not enough; for heavy traffic something more substantial than the 57 and 58 classes was needed, especially where the wartime 54 class had proved to be unsuitable as a basis for further development. A separate problem was fuel; during the war coal supply had deteriorated so seriously, that a partial return to wood fuel had to be made on the KUR, while on TR lines wood was still the common fuel over much of the network. It was generally felt that wood was only a poor substitute for higher-grade fuels, and some

Former TR ML class 2–8–2 No 2608 with Giesl ejector and air brakes, one of the last designs of the Tanganyika Railway, is seen here heading a goods train out of Tabora

engines, such as the MacArthurs, were very mediocre on it. Moreover coal imports from South Africa had been liable to disruption. Both wars had shown unpleasant examples of this and in the light of experience the EAR decided to take up oil burning again thus following earlier experiments dating back to the 1920s on such KUR classes as the EA and EB. Starting almost immediately all EAR engines were gradually converted to burn oil, a job which was completed by 1955.

The shortage of motive power was more difficult to overcome and the early 1950s was marked by intense design activity in the Nairobi drawing office. As a result several interesting designs were evolved, some of which never went beyond the drawing board. First was the pressing need for heavy motive power to cope with the upgoing traffic from Mombasa to Nairobi. One possible solution, doubling of the track, was found to be too costly in time and money, while even electrification at one stage was under serious consideration although ruled out on grounds of cost. Dieselisation at that time was still largely an unknown quantity except in North America, and elsewhere

steam locomotives remained supreme. It was with steam traction that EAR chose to continue. First thorough investigations were made as to the carrying capacity of the 80lb rail, with which the Mombasa-Nairobi line was laid at the time. The 28 class with its $17\frac{1}{2}$ ton axle loading had never given any trouble and as a result of careful investigation it was estimated that the track would even take twenty tons. Doubts were, however, expressed by the chief civil engineer on loadings which could be carried by the bridges. Nevertheless it was agreed that a new and extra heavy Garratt could be designed with an average axle loading of twenty tons and about 80,000lbs tractive effort, the projected locomotive received the preliminary classification 59. Detailed design work was left to Beyer Peacock after the specification had been drawn up and nine engines of the new type were ordered in 1950. Between then and the delivery of the first locomotives in 1955, the order grew to a total of thirty-four, for by this time traffic had more than doubled from the 1945 figure to 1,300 million ton-miles.

The 59s are the biggest, heaviest and most

No 5912 Mount Oldeani *differs from the other 59 4–8–2+2–8–4s in having an experimental blastpipe arrangement. Externally, it may be easily recognised by the smoke deflectors, another unique feature*

powerful steam locomotives in service anywhere in the world today, with a total weight of 252 tons, 83,350lb tractive effort and a total length over couplers of 104ft 1½in. They were designed to haul 1,200 ton trains on 1·5 per cent gradients and could do so at 14mph. By comparison, their immediate predecessors, the 58 class, could handle 700 tons on the same gradients at 10mph. Oil fuel consumption per mile averaged around 8·9 gallons for the 59s against 11·5 for the 58, which made the new giants the cheapest in oil consumption on the whole system in relation to the loads handled. Since the early 1960s, when the engines were fitted with Giesl ejectors, these figures, under test, became potentially even more favourable, but such figures unfortunately do not apply to normal in-service conditions.

The thirty-four engines of the 59 class, as supplied in 1955–6, have tapered axle loadings giving 19–21–21–19 tons on the coupled axles, the maximum that could be allowed on 80lb track. In the years between 1950, when they were conceived, and 1955 the main line had, however, been relaid with new 95lb rail east of Nairobi. This, incidentally, brought the EAR to an even more ambitious Garratt project, the proposed 61 class, which in the event did not materialise.

Some disadvantages had to be accepted in the design of the 59 as for various reasons it was not possible to build the engines with the flat-topped Belpaire firebox. The boilers in their present form, with a diameter of 7ft 6in, or more than twice the rail gauge, had already given Beyer Peacock some headaches in view of the limited loading gauge. The engines were built from the outset to burn oil, as were the older 58s, but, in case a return to coal should prove necessary, provision was made for a mechanical stoker, which in fact was never needed. In building the engines to the maximum weight allowed by the civil engineer no allowance had been made for adequately balancing the reciprocating masses, with the result that the 59s gave mechanical trouble in maintenance. Considerable vibration occurred in the speed range of 25 to 40 mph which led to many parts working loose. After a careful assessment of the design calculations showed, however, that twenty per cent reciprocating balance could be provided without incurring any restrictions by the civil engineer; modifications started in 1958, indeed stopped many of the troubles.

The locomotives were built with roller bearings on all axles and initially two different makes were used, Timken on the axles and Skefco/SKF on the big ends, but Skefco bearings were later replaced by Timken, one type being standardised. These massive locomotives naturally were built with bar frames and had power reversing gear.

After initial experiments with the Giesl ejector from 1957 a large-scale programme was initiated in the early 1960s to fit all post-war main-line engines with this equipment and the 59, bearing the brunt of heavy traffic, was one of the most important classes to be modified. One engine, No 5912 Mount Oldeani, experimentally received a different type of Giesl and also has a differently shaped chimney, and smoke deflectors on the smokebox. There has however been no marked difference in power output or fuel and water consumption but this is partly due to the fact that for some years No 5912 has been in the hands of two regular drivers. The author was told by the shed-master that the only difference with the other 59s is that lighting up 5912 is a more difficult and time-consuming job, but once in steam it is fully comparable with the rest of the class. Even before the Giesl fitting programme the 59 class did so well that congestion in Mombasa had long been cleared and traffic ran normally.

With a capacity of 2,700 gallons of oil and 8,600 gallons of water the 59s have reserves far beyond those of any other EAR locomotive. By comparison with previous Garratts the design of water tanks was modified; not only were they streamlined shape but were built with an inward slope towards the outer ends to improve visibility ahead. When the practice of name giving was resumed after the war, the 59s were nominated to receive names of East African tribes but as their restricted working area would have prevented most tribesmen from seeing them, it was decided instead to give them names of mountains. The tribal names were eventually given to the tender engines of classes 29, 30 and 31, which are in service on all parts of the system.

Today the 59 class locomotives are the mainstay of the heavy freight traffic between Mombasa and Nairobi, at which depots they are based. They are confined to this section because it was found, after all, that the 80lb rail, still laid between Nairobi and Nakuru, suffered too much from the heavy axle loads of the 59s to permit regular use.

On the long run to Nairobi of 330 miles the locomotives are worked on the caboose system, two regular crews taking over from each other at fixed points, to allow the other crew to rest in the caboose. But alas the 59's deep-throated bark is not going to last much more than a few years from

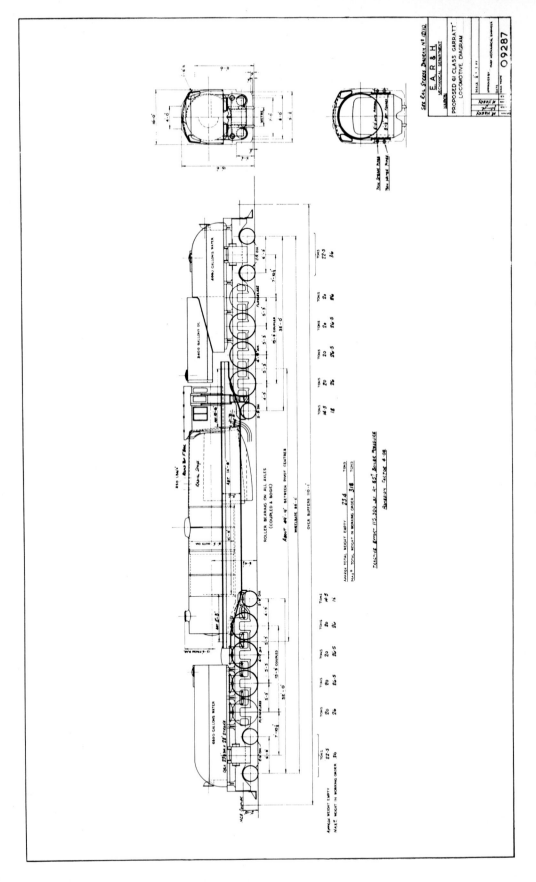

Drawing 7: Projected 61 class 4–8–2 + 2–8–4 Garratt locomotive

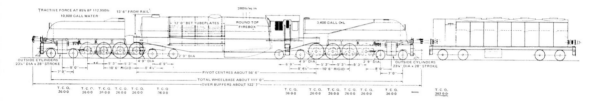

Drawing 8: Projected 61 class 4–8–4+4–8–4 Garratt locomotive, alternative version with condensing tender

now for by 1976 all steam power is scheduled to have disappeared from EAR lines.

Even before deliveries of the 59 class were complete the chief mechanical engineer, Bulman, had drawings prepared of an even larger Garratt, which should have been class 61, for the 60 class was already on order. The 61 design eclipsed any previous Garratt, including the 59, two possible versions were contemplated in the middle 1950s, a 4–8–2+2–8–4 and a 4–8–4+4–8–4 with a separate condensing tender. Both were designed with 4ft 9in driving wheels, compared with 4ft 6in for the 59, and no less than twenty-six tons axle load, which would have made them the largest narrow-gauge locomotives ever built! The 4–8–2+2–8–4 was estimated at 104ft 1in over the couplers, had a boiler diameter of 8ft 3in and would have developed 115,300lb tractive effort at an adhesion factor of 4·08. The giant would have had $23\frac{1}{2} \times 28$in cylinders and carried 3,400 gallons of oil and 10,600 gallons of water to feed its immense boiler, which was to be pressed at 250lb/sq in. Like the 59, this engine was designed with a round-top firebox.

The 4–8–4+4–8–4 version was even more interesting, featuring a condensing vehicle to allow longer runs. Condensing tenders once found favour in Europe, 0–10–0s being built by Swedish and German manufacturers for waterless areas in Russia. Some 4–8–2s with condensing equipment were also supplied shortly before World War II by German builders to Latin America, and during the war, when Germany occupied the western part of Russia, the type reappeared, but was not entirely successful, probably because of wartime maintenance conditions. Then, in 1952, Henschel designed a batch of 4–8–4s with condensing equipment for the South African Railways class 25 and it may well have been this project that commended itself to EAR in planning a condensing Garratt.

As drawn up, this 4–8–4+4–8–4 had an overall length of 122ft 7in without its tender, and an even

larger boiler diameter than that of the alternative concept, in this case 8ft 4in. Heating surface of the boiler tubes was 4,593sq ft, with 1,048sq ft of superheater surface, a tractive effort at 85 per cent boiler pressure of 112,950lb and water capacity of 10,800 gallons, all this making it even more superlative than the 4–8–2+2–8–4 project.

Both versions had flangeless wheels on the leading coupled axle of both power units; bar frames and MCB couplers were incorporated in the design, for the ABC couplers now in use are barely adequate for the 59's tractive effort! The 4–8–2+2–8–4 would have had a total weight of 318 tons, 210 of which was adhesive weight, while the comparable figures for the condensing version were 352 and 208 tons respectively.

In 1957, a third version of the 61 class was proposed; by that time, the idea of a condensing Garratt had been dropped and the 4–8–4+4–8–4 version was redesigned as a conventional Garratt. Overall dimensions in principle were retained, but the boiler and firebox were further increased in size. The coupled axles were given a tapered axle load in the same manner as the 59 class, the maximum calculated for this project being no less than 27 tons. With an 8ft 6in boiler diameter, 17ft 0in between the tubeplates and $23\frac{1}{2} \times 28$in cylinders this giant was expected to develop 115,000lb tractive effort at 85 per cent. The engine would have had 3,400 gallon oil capacity, 10,600 gallons of water, a round-top firebox and, predictably, roller bearings on all axles. Heating surfaces would have been 4,700sq ft for the boiler tubes, 380sq ft for the firebox, and 1,120sq ft for the superheater, giving a total of 6,200sq ft. This revised 4–8–4+4–8–4 was indeed an extraordinary proposal. In Bulman's own words, in a description for the East African Institution of Engineers: 'It (the 4–8–4+4–8–4) would have a boiler capacity of 70 per cent greater than the 59 class, and would haul a 1,800 ton load up the 1·5 per cent grade at

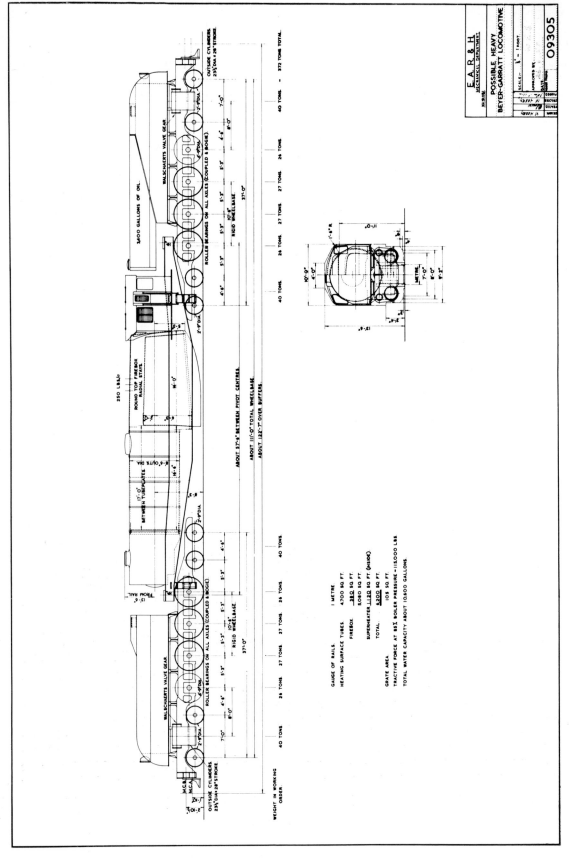

Drawing 9: Projected 61 class 4-8-4 + 4-8-4 Garratt locomotive, third version without condensing equipment

about 16mph, but would require a change in the type of coupling used and longer sidings, also bridge strengthening, all of which major operations would be uncalled for with dieselisation, to give equal traffic capacity. I am afraid, therefore, that the projected 61 class will never be built, but it was an interesting speculation to see just what could be done on the metre gauge track, and within our loading gauge dimensions into which it fits like a hand in a glove.'

The 61 class was indeed never built.

In the same family as the 59 and 61 classes belonged two projects for lighter Garratts, both 4–8–2+2–8–4s, one with 4ft 6in driving wheels and eighteen tons axle load, the other with 4ft and $16\frac{3}{4}$ tons respectively. Both were conceived on the same lines as the 59, but were generally lighter and had Belpaire fireboxes.

The 18 ton version originated in 1951 as a lighter counterpart to the 59, also featuring provision for a mechanical stoker, should conditions dictate a return to coal burning, in which case fifteen tons would be carried. It was designed to carry 2,800 gallons of oil and 6,600 gallons of water. The boiler was to work at a pressure of 200lb/sq in and had a diameter of 7ft 3in and a total heating surface of 3,676sq ft, making the ensemble a sizeable locomotive. It was supposed to

run at 50mph on 80lb track, and on the drawing set was referred to as 'engine E'. The $16\frac{3}{4}$ ton design, 'engine B', was more modest, although the boiler barrel was of the same dimensions to work at 210lb/sq in with a cylinder diameter of $18\frac{5}{8}$in, resulting in a calculated tractive effort of 65,350lb at 85 per cent boiler pressure, the same value as for 'engine E' with $19\frac{1}{4} \times 28$in cylinders. Both designs would have roller bearings on all axles. Another project drawn up at about the same time was for a 2–6–2+2–6–2 branch-line Garratt, more or less along the same lines as the engines that had been built for the Rhodesia Railways as class 14a.

As things turned out only one more Garratt class was to be built for the EAR besides the 59, and this was yet another development of the war-time 55 class. These engines, the 60 class, twenty-nine of which were built in 1953–4, differed only in minor respects from the 56s and the first twelve were in fact ordered as 5607–18. They have more water and less oil capacity, the only difference of any importance, and it was only just before delivery that it was decided to classify them separately. As EAR had requested early delivery and Beyer Peacock had an impressive quantity of orders at the time, the first twelve engines were sub-contracted to the Societe Franco-Belge at Raismes in France but the price is said to have been accord-

One of the Beyer Peacock-built class 60s, No 6017, during a test run direct from workshops in 1972

ingly high. Although they are one class, there are nevertheless some minor differences between the French- and the British-built 60s as a result.

With an axle load of only eleven tons, the 60 class is, with the 55 and 56 classes, the standard light Garratt on the system, taking all the lighter mixed traffic. It was on one of these engines, No 6029, that the first test with the Giesl ejector was made, No 5805 following suit. Today, all 60s have this equipment. Originally the 60 class carried the names of the Governors of Kenya, Tanganyika and Uganda, but later the nameplates were removed. At present, only No 6001 still carries a name *Umoja* (=Unity). They are straightforward engines, with the well-tried Belpaire firebox, a working pressure of 200lb/sq in and 16×24in cylinders, developing a tractive effort of 43,520lb. They, too, have roller bearings on all axles, but somewhat surprisingly plate frames of wartime origin were retained, like the 55 and 56 classes. Although the 60s are quite good engines, they never came came up to the level of the 56s, especially where the free steaming quality of the boilers is concerned.

In the field of tank engines a heavy 0–8–0T was considered for shunting work in the late 1940s as class 13, but before the first engine was ordered the design was altered to include carrying wheels. This was done not only to improve its riding qualities but also to increase its bunker capacity; eventually the engines were supplied by North British in 1953 as 4–8–2 tanks. The design was said to have been adapted from a 4–10–2T engine built early in the century for the Natal Government Railway in South Africa. These locomotives were later rebuilt as 4–8–2Ts and as such fifty years later served as the prototype for the EAR 13 class. The fact that a pair of coupled wheels had been left out resulted in very uneven weight distribution and the axle load was particularly excessive on the trailing pony truck. In consequence the 13s as supplied were by no means ideal locomotives, being prone to frequent derailments in sidings. This was the main reason behind the EAR's decision to convert them to 4–8–4Ts and the trailing ponies were changed to bogies recovered from old 50 class Garratts then in process of withdrawal. Although the wheel diameters are the same, the old-type wheels on the rear bogie clearly show that some form of rebuilding was carried out on these engines. At the same time the side tanks were extended and lined up with the smokebox door, which necessitated the repositioning of the compressor, while the rear fuel tank was also enlarged slightly. In this

North British-built 4–8–2T No 1301 as supplied in 1953

Engine No 1307 at Voi shed, showing the extent to which the class was rebuilt with the 4–8–4T wheel arrangement and longer tanks

altered form the 13s became useful engines and at the time of writing all are still hard at work, not being due for replacement for some years to come.

Besides the 13 class, there were other projects for eight-coupled tank engines in the early 1950s. One was for a 4–8–4T suburban locomotive, the other, proposed as class 14, was for a 2–8–4T for shunting work on 50lb track. Featuring a shortened version of the 31 class boiler, and with a maximum axle load of 13·8 tons this project was still under consideration in 1953. The boiler was designed for a working pressure of 200lb/sq in and with 17 × 26in cylinders and 54 tons of adhesive weight a tractive effort of 26,600lb was envisaged. Their chances were spoilt by the diesel; results with

lighter diesel shunters showed that greater tractive effort at lower fuel consumption could be expected, and diesel shunters were in fact placed in service in 1956 as class 84 (now 44).

The project for the 4–8–4T suburban locomotive did not fare any better; it was designed to have about 42 tons of adhesive weight, 200lb/sq in working pressure like the 14 class (the 13s have only 180lb) and 4ft driving wheels. On the drawing they are handsome, although one wonders whether suburban traffic has ever been sufficiently developed to warrant special locomotives, which, as tanks, would have had restricted bunker capacity. The only suburban traffic since the way has been between Mombasa and Mazeras, unless Kisumu-

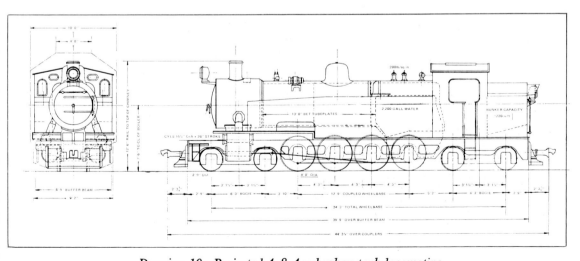

Drawing 10: Projected 4–8–4 suburban tank locomotive

Class 29 2–8–2 No 2923, one of the batch of 11 1955-built locomotives seen here at Nakuru shed in December 1971

Butere is also considered as such, and it seems more likely that the engines would have wandered off in shunting duties together with the 13s. The project was discontinued, and the suburban 4–8–4T never appeared.

We now come to the last tender locomotives to be built for the East African, classes 29, 30 and 31. With the 59 class Garratts, they were at the same time the last steam locomotives built for EAR.

The 29 class 2–8–2s were the first new tender locomotives to see service on the Kenya-Uganda main line since the introduction of the heavy mail class 28 locomotives in 1928. They were derived from the Nigerian Railways 2–8–2 River class, which is indeed similar, except that it was built to burn low-grade coal compared with oil on the EAR engines. This similarity is the reason why the 29s are sometimes called the 'Nigerian' engines by the

crews. The first two were supplied by North British in 1951, and eighteen more followed during 1952. With an axle load of thirteen tons the 29 class is intended for freight trains on main lines and in this category has proved itself to be a reliable and good design, so much so even, that in 1955 eleven additional engines were obtained from North British. These newer locomotives differ from the earlier ones in that they have spring-loaded intermediate buffing gear, later standardised on the 31 class 2–8–4s, and larger injectors than the first twenty engines. Externally, they are easily distinguishable for a larger smokebox door has been fitted than on the earlier engines. To reduce the weight on the trailing pony truck, already heavily stressed by the big Belpaire firebox, the compressors were repositioned to be in line with the smokebox door, and in consequence some minor changes had to be introduced to the leading pony truck.

The only other important change was the introduction of Giesl ejectors in the 1960s, giving the engines more power yet reducing the fuel consumption rate. The Giesl equipment itself demands careful driving and maintenance which tends to cancel out some operational advantages. In general, locomotives with Giesl ejectors should be driven with about five per cent less regulator in comparison to non-Giesl engines to be most effective and accord with the principles of Dr Giesl-Gieslingen the inventor of the device. The Giesl ejectors had an unfortunate side effect for the greater train loads and tighter schedules permitted to Giesl fitted engines resulted in difficulties with some of the older classes, for example the 57s and 58s; they had always been somewhat underboilered and now deteriorated rapidly. In all cases of withdrawal, boiler troubles were the cause and it may thus, in a sense, be said that indirectly 'the Giesl killed the 58'.

The somewhat disappointing effects of the ejector were partly due to the fact that the original tests were carried out on engines that had just come out of works and were thus in optimal maintenance condition, while being driven during the test runs by the best drivers. These non-representative trials more or less automatically led to an over-optimistic assessment of the potential of Giesl fitted locomotives. Moreover, driving standards have unfortunately not been maintained at the same level since then. These circumstances cannot be ignored and the present chief mechanical engineer told the author that he was not sure whether he would have introduced the ejectors at all!

As mentioned above, a point of some concern in the design of the 29 class was the relatively high axle load on the trailing pony, which caused the engines to lean back with heavy trains, with consequent loss of adhesive weight. To remedy this shortcoming, the EAR went in following designs to a wheel arrangement with a bogie under the firebox, considered by many engineers to be the best possible solution for locomotives with a big and heavy firebox, as it improves riding and, indirectly, eases maintenance. The 2–8–4s thus evolved belong to two classes, 30 and 31, introduced in 1955–6 and built by North British and Vulcan, respectively. The 30 class is the heavier of the two and is directly derived from the 29, featuring the same boiler, although adhesive weight is slightly less as a result of the introduction of the bogie under the firebox. The bogie has American-inspired cast steel outside frames and was introduced following the example of the Canadian Pacific type 59 to improve riding. For the same reason, compensated spring gear on the coupled axles was reintroduced following the example of the pre-war 28 class Mikados. These changes certainly resulted in better riding qualities for both classes.

Another novel feature of the 30 class is its big tender, running on six-wheel bogies, also of cast steel and having a capacity of 1,950 gallons of fuel oil and 7,000 gallons of water. This, with Timken roller bearings throughout has resulted in an engine capable of running long distances over the Central Line of Tanzania, on sections with unreliable water supplies, like Morogoro-Tabora. At present, the 29 and 31 classes are working from

North British 2–8–4 No 3011 Luguru *just outshopped at Nairobi in July 1972*

81

Class 31 2–8–4 No 3103 Uganda *heads an up goods train on the main line east of Nairobi*

different sheds in all three countries, but the 30s are an all-Tanzania class.

For branch-line work Vulcan supplied a generally similar but lighter 2–8–4 as class 31. It has a smaller boiler and cylinders to result in a lighter axle load of only 11 tons. The tender, too, is lighter than that of the 30 class and reverted to the pre-war system of rigid axles instead of bogies; the tenders are much smaller and have a tapered axle load, allowing for 4,108 gallons of water and

1,667 gallons of oil. Common to both 30 and 31 classes are the 4ft wheel diameter and the fact that both carry names of East African tribes. On both classes, too, the diameter of the trailing bogie wheels is different from the front the former being 2ft 9in and the latter 2ft 4½in.

With the delivery of the last 30, 31 and 59 class locomotives in 1956, the development of steam power in East Africa came to an end, and the future was turned over to diesel traction with,

Nairobi shed at night, a picture taken in January 1972

in the long run, possibly electrification. Many steam engines are still at work and at the time of writing about two thirds of the total locomotive stock is steam. But large-scale scrapping is to begin shortly and it is expected that the last active steam locomotives will be retired by 1976. The latest classes will not have the longest life as about thirty to thirty-five 4–8–0s of class 24, dating back to the 1920s are scheduled to be kept as a reserve for emergencies, but all other types are to be scrapped during the next four to five years.

Fortunately, the EAR is planning to keep a number of steam locomotives for its railway museum, and thus an impression of what steam was like in this part of the world will be preserved for posterity, for the fourth quarter of the twentieth century is almost certain to witness the final death of steam power on the world's railways.

EAST AFRICAN RAILWAYS, 1949–1956

Class	Wheel arrangement	Builders	Running numbers
12	2–6–2T	Bagnall 2901–2, 1950	1201–2
13	4–8–2T/ 4–8–4T	NBL 27060–77, 1953	1301–18
26	2–8–2	Vulcan 6182–7 ⎫ 1952 Stephenson & Hawthorns 7444–9 ⎭	2607–12
27	2–8–2	Alco (2716) ⎫ Baldwin (2711–15) ⎬ 1944 Davenport (2709–10) ⎭ DSM workshops (2717) 1953	2709–17
29	2–8–2	NBL 26905–20 ⎫ 1951–2 27085–8 ⎭ 27436–46 1955	2901–20 2921–31
30	2–8–4	NBL 27447–68, 27474–7, 1955	3001–26
31	2–8–4	Vulcan 6228–73, 1955	3101–46
55	4–8–2+2–8–4	Beyer Peacock 7155, 7154, 7149 ⎫ 1945 71 , 7148, ⎭	5507–11
59	4–8–2+2–8–4	Beyer Peacock 7632–58, 7700–6, 1955	5901–34
60	4–8–2+2–8–4	Franco-Belge* ⎫ 7565–80, 7659–66, 7721–5, 1953–4 Beyer Peacock ⎭	6001–29

  * 6001–12 built under subcontract by Franco-Belge; Beyer Peacock numbers allocated, original Fr-B numbers 2983–94.

STEAM LOCOMOTIVES OF EAST AFRICAN RAILWAYS

TR/KUR locomotive renumbering list

(locomotives taken over by EAR in 1948)

EAR numbers	Wheel arrangement	Old class		Old numbers
1001–8	2–6–4T	KUR	EE	61–8/91–8/391–8
1101–4 ⎫	2–6–2T	TR	ST	11–14/103–6
1105–31 ⎬	2–6–2T	KUR	ED1	10–36/310–36
1201–2	2–6–2T	TR	SS	–
1301–18	4–8–2T/4–8–4T	–		–
2001–4	4–6–0	TR	BB	270–3
2101–8	4–8–2	TR	RV	250–7/500–7
2201–4	4–8–0	TR	NZ	1095–8/200–3
2205–17	4–8–0	TR	G	20–32/204–16
2218–23	4–8–0	KUR	EB1	128–61 (less scrapped ones)
2301–6	4–8–0	TR	DL	200–5/300–5
2401–62	4–8–0	KUR	EB3	162–223
2501–11	2–8–2	TR	MK	206–16/400–10
2601–06 ⎫	2–8–2	TR	ML	700–05/600–05
2607–12 ⎬	2–8–2	–		–
2701–8 ⎫	2–8–2	TR	MR	800–7
2709–17 ⎬	2–8–2	–		–
2801–6	2–8–2	KUR	EA	1–6
2901–31	2–8–2	–		–
3001–26	2–8–4	·		–
3101–46	2–8–4	–		–
5001–18	4–8–2+2–8–4	KUR	EC1	45–64 (less nos 51 and 53, sold to Indo-China)
5101–2	4–8–2+2–8–4	KUR	EC1	65–6
5201–10	4–8–2+2–8–4	KUR	EC2	67–76
5301–2	4–8–2+2–8–4	TR	GA	700–2 (702 scrapped 1944)
5401–7	4–8–2+2–8–4	KUR	EC4	89–95/100–6
5501– 2 ⎫	4–8–2+2–8–4	KUR	EC5	120–1
5503– 6 ⎬	4–8–2+2–8–4	TR	GB	750–3
5507–11 ⎭	4–8–2+2–8–4	–		–
5601–6	4–8–2+2–8–4	KUR	EC6	122–7
5701–12	4–8–4+4–8–4	KUR	EC3	77–88
5801– 7 ⎫	4–8–4+4–8–4	KUR	EC3	89–95
5808–18 ⎬	4–8–4+4–8–4	–		–
5901–34	4–8–2+2–8–4	–		–
6001–29	4–8–2+2–8–4	–		–

No new EAR–numbers:

–	0–4–0T	TR	ST	1–8/51–8
–	2–8–0T	TR	GT	101–2 (ex-German series UE 11–14)

APPENDICES

APPENDIX 1

Leading Particulars of Locomotives

GERMAN EAST AFRICA

Class	Type	Boiler Pressure (atm)	Grate area (sq m)	Heating surface (sq m)				Cylinders (mm)	Coupled wheel dia (mm)	Weights (tons)		Tractive effort (kp, at 60%)	Capacity	
				Tubes	Fire-box	Super-heater	Total			Maximum	Adhesive		water (m3)	Fuel (ton)
Usambara Eisenbahn														
B1 T	0-4-2T	12	0·6	38·3		—		280 × 420	920	19·6		2577		
B'+B T	0-4-4-0T	12	1	43·3		—		HP 250 × 400 / LP 380 × 400	820	26·4	26·4	5325	3·2	2·5 m3 wood
1'D T	2-8-0T	12	1·3	62·5		—		370 × 500	1000	37·0	30·0	4500	4·4	3·2 „ „
1'D	2-8-0	12	1·8	83·6		—		370 × 500	1000	35·0	28·0	4930	12	7 „ „
OAEG														
B T	0-4-0T	12	0·6	27·7		—		260 × 400	800	16·5	16·5	2480	2	0·6 / 0·3 m3 oil
B T	0-4-0T	10	0·4	23·4		—		HP 240 × 400 / LP 260 × 500	800	12	12	1725	1·25	0·5
B'+B T	0-4-4-0T	12	1·2	53·7		—		HP 240 × 400 / LP 260 × 500	950	30·0	30·0	5800	4·0	1·2
(1B)+B T	2-4-4-0T	14	1·3	68·1		—		HP 390 × 500 / LP 445 × 500	950	45·0	37·5	9480	6·0	2·2
D1'T	0-8-2T	12	1·4	70·5		—		390 × 500	1000	39·5	32·5	5500	5·5	4·0 m3 wood
1'D T	2-8-0T	12	1·3	62·5		—		370 × 500	1000	40·0	34·0	4500	5·0	4·0 „ „
1'D T	2-8-0T	12	1·3	65·1 (Borsig) / 62·5 (O&K) / 61·8 (others)		—		370 × 500	1000	39·0	34·0	5000 (Borsig) / 4500 (O&K) / 4930 (orhers)	5·0	4·0 „ „
			1·2							38·5 (Hanomag)	33·4			
1'D	2-8-0	12	2·6	127·5		—		430 × 540	1000	46·2	39·1	7190	15·0	10·0 „ „

85

UGANDA RAILWAY/KENYA-UGANDA RAILWAY

Class	Type	Boiler Pressure (lb sq in)	Grate area (sq ft)	Heating surface (sq ft) tubes	firebox	superheater	total	Cylinders (in)	Coupled wheel dia ft in	Weights (tons) maximum	adhesive	Tractive effort (lb, at 85%)	Capacity water (gal)	fuel (cu ft)
A	2-4-0T	120	5·7	327·1	36·2		363·3	10 ×16	3 – 6	16·5		3857	400 (450)	50 (45)
E	0-4-2	140	7·2	386·2	50		436·2	11½×17	3 – 0	16		6557	1000	80
N	2-6-0	140	10·1	509	57		566	14 ×20	3 – 0	34·9 (in tender)		12950	1200	1½ tons
F	0-6-0	160	13	670·9	79·8		750·7	14½×20	3 – 6¼	30·1	30·1	13460	1500	2·3 „
B	2-6-0	160	12·7	508·1	71·1		579·2	14½×20	3 – 5½	29·0	24·8	13780	1500	2·7 „
MT	0-6-6-0	180	32	1398	115		1513	HP15½×20 LP24½×20	3 – 3	60·3	60·3	27500	2140 (3050)	6 „
ED	2-6-2T	160	12·8	926	100		1026	15 ×22	3 – 7	44·9	29·6	15650	800	1½ „
EE	2-6-4T	160	12·8	926	98		1024	15 ×22	3 – 7	52·4	30·0	14470	1200	250
ED1	2-6-2T	160 (165)	12·8	(900) 926 (900)	100		(998) 1026 (1000)	(16 ×22) 15 ×22	3 – 7	50·7	33·8 (34·5)	16150	1200	(760 gals oil) 2½ tons (1033 gals oil)
EB	4-8-0	180	17·5	1017	126		1143	16 ×22	3 – 7	42·3	34·2	20040	2140	240
EB1	4-8-0	180	17·5	1017 (1039)	126		1143 (1165)	16 ×22	3 – 7	42·3	34·2	20040	2140	240
EB2	4-8-0	160	17·5	724	126	167	1017	17 ×22	3 – 7	42·4	33·5	20100	2500	(1500 gals oil) 4½ tons
EB3	4-8-0	165	19·1	900	140	152	1192	18 ×22	3 – 7	48·1	39·4 (40·1)	23249	2500 (3500)	6 (9½ tons) (1900 gals oil)
EA	2-8-2	180	40·5	1401 (2107)	180	729 (574)	2310 (2861)	21¼×28	4 – 3	90·7	69·5	37938	5000	12 tons (2375 gals oil)
EC	4-8-2+2-8-4	170	43·6	1863	174	380	2417	16½×22	3 – 7	125·4	79·4	40252	4250	6 tons
EC1	4-8-2+2-8-4	170	43·6	1863	174	380	2417	16½×22	3 – 7	130·9	83·9	40255	5250	6 „
EC2	4-8-2+2-8-4	170 (180)	43·6	1856	194	380	2430	16½×22	3 – 7	142·1	88·0	42600	5250	2375 gals oil
EC3	4-8-4+4-8-4	220 (225)	48·5	1963	169	429	2561	16 ×26	4 – 6	186·2	97·0	47200	6000	2375 „ „
EC4	4-8-2+2-8-4	180	51·3	2310	212	470	2992	19 ×24	3 – 9¼	171·5	112·0	58260	6000	2375 „ „
EC5	4-8-2+2-8-4	200	48·8	1800	183	399	2382	16 ×24	4 – 0	133·4	83·7	43520	4590	1200 „ „
EC6	4-8-2+2-8-4	200	48·8	1753	164	370	2287	16 ×24	4 – 0	146·8	88·0	43520	4200	2382 „ „

TANGANYIKA RAILWAY

Class	Type	Boiler pressure (lb sq in)	Grate area (sq ft)	Heating surface (sq ft)				Cylinders (in)	Coupled wheel (dia) (ft in)	Weights (tons)		Tractive effort (lb, at 85%)	Capacity	
				tubes	firebox	superheater	total			maximum	adhesive		water (gal)	fuel (cu ft)
War-imported locomotives														
F	0-6-0	140	12·5	583	59	—	642	14 ×20	3-6½	22·0	22·0	9684	1500	210
G (ABR)	4-8-0	180	17·5	1166	126	—	1292	16 ×22	3-7	40·1	32·2	20037	2000	3 tons
G (NGSR)	4-8-0	180	17·5	1047	126	—	1173	16 ×22	3-7	40·7	32·6	20036	2500	208 "
M	2-6-0	160	14	738	82	—	820	14 ×20	3-6½	24	20·2	9680	1200	4½ tons
TR locomotives														
DL	4-8-0	160 (165)	18·3	945	129	249	1323	18 ×23	3-7	49·8	37·7	24300	2500	2019 gal oil
MK	2-8-2	160 (165)	27	1306	139	297	1742	18 ×23	3-7	57·7	40·1	24300	3500	1300 "
G	4-8-0	180	17·5	1047	126	—	1173	16 ×22	3-7	41·4	32·9	20040	2500	1900 "
RV	4-8-2	160 (165)	27	1306	139	297	1742	18 ×23	3-7	59·8	39·8	24300	3500	1300 "
ST	2-6-2T	160 (165)	12·8	926 (900)	100	—	1026 (1000)	15 ×22	3-7	50·7 (53·9)	33·8 (34·5)	16150	1200	1033 "
GA	4-8-2+2-8-4	170 (180)	43·6	1856	194	380	2430	16½×22	3-7	138·3	83·8	42600	4925	2455 "
GB	4-8-2+2-8-4	200	48·8	1800	183	399	2382	16 ×24	4-0	133·4	83·7	43520	4590	1200 "
ML	2-8-2	180	27	1272	139	321	1731	17½×23	3-7	51·8	39·0	25050	4200	1300 "
MR	2-8-2	180	27·8	1247	115	374	1736	16 ×24	4-0	52·0	35·7	19550	4166	1350 "
BB	4-6-0	160	22·2	745	83	219	1056	16½×22	4-0	39·1	29·7	16969	3000	4½ tons

EAST AFRICAN RAILWAYS

Class	Type	Boiler pressure (lb sq in)	Grate area (sq ft)	Heating surface (sq ft)				Cylinders (in)	Coupled wheel dia ft in	Weights (tons)		Tractive effort (lb, at 85%)	Capacity	
				tubes	firebox	superheater	total			maximum	adhesive		water (gal)	fuel (gal)
12	2-6-2T	180	12·8	706	100	181	987	16 ×22	3-7	54·4	35·1	20040	1500	800
13	4-8-2T / 4-8-4T	180	25	878	110	220	1208	19 ×24	3-9½	86·5	51·7	29134	2935	805
29	2-8-2	200	38	1680	146	446	2272	18 ×26	4-0	73·8	52·0	29835	4800	2056
30	2-8-4	200	38	1680	146	446	2272	18 ×26	4-0	77·7	51·2	29835	7000	1950
31	2-8-4	200	30	1511	124	328	1963	17 ×26	4-0	70·2	45·0	26600	4108	1667
58	4-8-4+4-8-4	225	48·5	1963	169	429	2561	16½×26	4-6	186·3	94·0	50200	6000	2375
59	4-8-2+2-8-4	225	72	3290	247	747	4284	20½×28	4-6	251·7	159·5	83350	8600	2700
60	4-8-2+2-8-4	200	48·8	1729	170	370	2269	16 ×24	4-0	152·3	86·9	43520	4612	1800

APPENDIX 2
Locomotive Names

Locomotive Names	Name	Number	Remarks
1: German East Africa			
Usambara Eisenbahn:			
Nos 6–10 (0–4–4–0T Mallet)	*Deutschland*	6	
	Preussen	7	
		8	
		9	
		10	
2: Kenya-Uganda Railway			
EA class (2–8–2)	*Mvita*	1	EAR 2801
	Shimanzi	2	2802
	Vanga	3	2803
	Kilifi	4	2804
	Lamu	5	2805
	Malindi	6	2806
EC1 class (4–8–2+2–8–4)		45	EAR 5001
		46	5002
	Toro	47	5003
	Masai	48	5004
	Nyanzi	49	5005
	Meru	50	5006
		51	sold to Yunnan Rly
	Masaka	52	5007
		53	sold to Yunnan Rly
	Nandi	54	EAR 5008
	Bunyoro	55	5009
		56	5010
	Kikuyu	57	5011
	Ankole	58	5012
		59	5013
		60	5014
		61	5015
	Londiani	62	5016
	Ukamba	63	5017
	Machakos	64	5018
EC1 class (1930)	*Laikipia*	65	5101
		66	5102
EC2 class (4–8–2+2–8–4)	*Busoga*	67	5201
	Kavirondo	68	5202
	Mubendi	69	5203
	Turkhana	70	5204
	Nyeri	71	5205
	Kiambu	72	5206
	Nzoia	73	5207
	Isiolo	74	5208
	Nakuru	75	5209
	Entebbe	76	5210
EC3 class (4–8–4+4–8–4)	*Mengo*	77	5701
	Teso	78	5702
	Uasingishu	79	5703
	Narok	80	5704
	Marakwet	81	5705
	Wajir	82	5706
	Chua	83	5707
	Gulu	84	5708
	Lango	85	5709
	Budama	86	5710
	Karamoja	87	5711
	Kigezi	88	5712
3: Tanganyika Railway			
RV class (4–8–2)	*Kalambo*	250/500	EAR 2101
	Ruvuma	251/501	2102
	Rufiji	252/502	2103
	Pangani	253/503	2104
	Ruaha	254/504	2105

	Kagera	255/505	2106
	Lukuedi	256/506	2107
	Lupa	257/507	2108
GA class (4–8–2+2–8–4)	*Arusha*	300/700	5301
	Iringa	301/701	5302
	Bukoba	302/702	scrapped 1944

4 : East African Railways

29 class (2–8–2)	*Boran*	2901	'Tribal' class
	Bukusu	2902	
	Bunyore	2903	
	Chuka	2904	
	Digo	2905	scrapped 1972
	Dorobo	2906	
	Duruma	2907	
	Elgeyo	2908	
	Embu	2909	
	Galla	2910	
	Giriyama	2911	
	Kakamega	2912	
	Tuken★	2913	formerly *Kamasia★*
	Kamba	2914	
	Kikuyu	2915	
	Kipsigis	2916	
	Kisii	2917	
	Luo	2918	
	Maragoli	2919	
	Marakwet	2920	
	Masai of Kenya	2921	
	Meru of Kenya	2922	
	Magodo	2923	
	Nandi	2924	
	Nyika	2925	
	Samburu	2926	
	Suk	2927	
	Taveta	2928	
	Teita	2929	
	Tiriki	2930	
	Turkana	2931	
30 class (2–8–4)	*Tanganyika★*	3001	'Tribal' class formerly *Arusha★*
	Bena	3002	
	Bondei	3003	
	Chagga	3004	
	Gogo	3005	
	Ha	3006	
	Haya	3007	
	Hehe	3008	
	Iramba	3009	
	Irakwu	3010	
	Luguru	3011	
	Makonde	3012	
	Makua	3013	
	Masai of Tanganyika	3014	
	Meru of Tanganyika	3015	
	Mwera	3016	
	Ngindo	3017	
	Nyakyusa	3018	
	Nyamwezi	3019	
	Nyaturu	3020	
	Pare	3021	
	Pogoro	3022	
	Sambaa	3023	
	Sukuma	3024	
	Zaramo	3025	
	Zigua	3026	
31 class (2–8–4)	*Baganda*	3101	'Tribal' class
	Batoro	3102	
	Uganda★	3103	formerly *Acholi★*
	Alur	3104	

Bagisu	3105	
Bagwe	3106	
Bagwere	3107	
Bahehe	3108	
Bahororo	3109	
Bakiga	3110	
Bakoki	3111	
Bakonjo	3112	
Bamba	3113	
Banyala	3114	
Banyankore	3115	
Banyaruanda	3116	
Banyoro	3117	
Banyuli	3118	
Basamia	3119	
Basese	3120	
Basoga	3121	
Batwa	3122	
Bavuma	3123	
Chope	3124	
Dodoth	3125	
Jie	3126	
Jonam	3127	
Jopadhola	3128	
Kakwa	3129	
Karamojong	3130	
Kenyi	3131	
Kumam	3132	
Lang'o	3133	
Lugbara	3134	
Madi	3135	
Sebei	3136	
Iteso	3137	
Upe	3138	
Pokomo	3139	
Rendille	3140	
Ribe	3141	
Sanye	3142	
Somal	3143	
Tharaka	3144	
Tsoto	3145	
Wamia	3146	
59 class (4–8–2＋2–8–4)	*Mount Kenya*	5901
	Ruwenzori Mountains	5902
	Mount Meru	5903
	Mount Elgon	5904
	Mount Muhavura	5905
	Mount Sattima	5906
	Mount Kinangop	5907
	Mount Loolmalasin	5908
	Mount Mgahinga	5909
	Mount Hanang	5910
	Mount Sekerri	5911
	Mount Oldeani	5912	with smoke deflectors
	Mount Debasien	5913
	Mount Londiani	5914
	Mount Mtorwi	5915
	Mount Rungwe	5916
	Mount Kitumbeine	5917
	Mount Gelai	5918
	Mount Lengai	5919
	Mount Mbeya	5920
	Mount Nyiru	5921
	Mount Blackett	5922
	Mount Longonot	5923
	Mount Eburu	5924
	Mount Monduli	5925
	Mount Kimhandu	5926
	Mount Tinderet	5927
	Mount Kilimanjaro	5928
	Mount Longido	5929
	Mount Shengena	5930
	Ulguru Mountains	5931

	Ol'donyo Sabuk	5932	
	Mount Suswa	5933	
	Menengai Crater	5934	
60 class (4–8–2 + 2–8–4)	Sir Geoffrey Archer⋆	6001	renamed Umoja⋆
	Sir Hesketh Bell	6002	60 class no longer
	Sir Stewart Symes	6003	named except 6001
	Sir Frederick Jackson	6004	
	Sir Bernard Bourdillon	6005	
	Sir Harold MacMichael	6006	
	Sir Mark Young	6007	
	Sir Wilfred Jackson	6008	
	Sir Edward Twining	6009	
	Sir Donald Cameron	6010	
	Sir William Battershill	6011	
	Sir Percy Girouard	6012	
	Sir Henry Belfield	6013	
	Sir Joseph Byrne	6014	
	Sir Robert Brooke-Popham	6015	
	Sir Henry Moore	6016	
	Sir John Hall	6017	
	Sir Charles Dundas	6018	
	Sir Philip Mitchell	6019	
	Sir Evelyn Baring	6020	
	Sir William Gowers	6021	
	Sir Andrew Cohen	6022	
	Sir Edward Northey	6023	
	Sir James Hayes-Sadler	6024	
	Sir Henry Colville	6025	scrapped
	Sir Horace Byatt	6026	
	Sir Gerald Portal	6027	
	Sir H. H. Johnston	6028	
	Sir Edward Grigg	6029	

APPENDIX 3
Locomotive Liveries

ALTHOUGH it is not possible in this book to go into minute livery details it will be useful to summarise as a general impression the colours in which the locomotives were and are finished. The most difficult in this respect are the former German engines, for reliable colour pictures of them do not exist, and scarcely anybody remembers such details well over half a century after German rule ended in East Africa. It is not improbable, however, that the locomotives were painted green, in the same fashion as many engines in Germany itself. During British times in Tanganyika German engines that had been salvaged were graphited, but they are unlikely to have been so during German ownership.

Midland red—a crimson lake colour known by that name from its use by the Midland Railway in Britain—was used by the later Tanganyika Railway (TR), where it was introduced in the early 1920s. This colour was also in use for passenger coaches. Some engines, notably Garratts, were painted black, however, at least during the period immediately before the amalgamation in 1948. The Uganda Railway (UR), from 1926 the Kenya-Uganda Railway (KUR), graphited all its engines, which resulted in a silvery grey finish. This should not be confused with grey-and-black paintwork—photographic grey—in which the engines were often supplied by the builders and which is shown on works photographs. On the KUR engines, only the smokeboxes and buffer beams were painted, black and bright red respectively.

Two special occasions brought a temporary change to KUR locomotives; for the occasion of the visit of the Duke and Duchess of York in December 1924 one of the new oil-burning 4–8–0s of class EB3, No 179, was painted black. This engine was also equipped with electric light, the first locomotive on the UR to receive this equipment. The other exception was a 4–8–2+2–8–4 Garratt of class EC1, No 50, painted maroon for the occasion of the visit of the Prince of Wales in September 1928. In both cases, the engines were painted only for the particular occasion, reverting to the normal graphite-and-black afterwards.

Numbers on the UR/KUR engines were in usually independent brass figures riveted or screwed on, and the railway's initials were in big brass letters riveted to the tender sides or on the bunker in the case of tank engines. There were exceptions, however, and some engines had both numbers and initials painted when delivered. In other cases,

drivers embellished their engines with oval brass number plates taken off passenger coaches numbered similarly to locomotives. The photograph on page 34 shows Mallet engine No 114 with such a plate, in this case taken off a second-class coach.

The TR used such oval number plates as standard and had its initials painted, in semi-relief style lettering, on the tender or bunker sides. As the engines were painted instead of graphited, painted numbers and lettering was reasonably durable. The German engines on the Usambara Eisenbahn, the present Tanga line, in general had square number plates and a long rectangular plate reading 'Usambara Eisenbahn'. On some engines a third plate was carried with the German eagle. The first locomotives on this line were different for they had number and owner's plate combined on one square plate on both sides of the smokebox reading EGFDOA-UE, for Eisenbahn Gesellschaft für Deutsch-Ostafrika-Usambara Eisenbahn, plus the engine's number.

In contrast, on the Central Line the engines mostly had a combined owner's/number plate on the cab sides or the smokebox, but here again there were exceptions to the rule, as in the case of a class of 0–4–4–0T Mallets which had their numbers in the UR style of loose brass figures. The *Reichsadler* was omitted from the OAEG locomotives.

After the amalgamation of KUR and TR into EAR in 1948, the TR-red was generally introduced by the new CME Mr G. Gibson, during the 1950s; this colour scheme is still in use. Locomotives are painted maroon with black smokeboxes and black-and-yellow lining, stainless steel or silver-painted boiler bands, black frames and bright red buffer beams. Brass number plates are rectangular in shape, with figures and rim polished or sometimes painted yellow, on a bright red background. The lettering EAR has been kept in the old KUR style. There used to be slight differences between locomotives shopped at Nairobi works and those from Dar es Salaam; Dar es Salaam employed a more elaborately painted style, with black-and-yellow trimming on boiler bands, cylinders and on the sides of the running boards, and in the bright African sun an engine ex-works from Dar es Salaam was a marvellous sight. Since early 1972, however, heavy repairs to steam locomotives have been concentrated at Nairobi and consequently the beautiful Dar es Salaam livery is gradually dying out.

ABBREVIATIONS

Both in the text and in the tables in this book abbreviations have been used to avoid unnecessary repetition. The full titles of the most important ones are given below:

ABC	Automatic Buffer Coupler
ABR	Assam Bengal Railway
BB & CI	Bombay, Baroda & Central India Railway
BESA	British Engineering Standards Association
BP	Beyer, Peacock & Co Ltd, Gorton Foundry, Manchester
BR	Burma Railway
DKEBBG	Deutsche Kolonial Eisenbahn Bau- und Betriebs Gesellschaft
DSM	Dar es Salaam
EARC	East African Railways Corporation (since 1969)
EAR & H	East African Railways & Harbours (until 1969)
EGFDOA-UE	Eisenbahn Gesellschaft Für Deutsch-Ost Afrika-Usambara Eisenbahn
Fr-B	Societe Franco-Belge de Materiel de Chemins de Fer, Raismes, France
GIP	Great Indian Peninsula Railway
Hanomag	Hannover'sche Maschinenbau A G, vormals Georg Egestorff, Hannover-Linden
KUR	Kenya-Uganda Railway
MSM	Madras & Southern Mahratta Railway
NBL	North British Locomotive Company Ltd, Hyde Park Works, Glasgow
NGSR	Nizam's Guaranteed State Railway
OAEG	Ost-Afrikanische Eisenbahn Gesellschaft
O & K	Orenstein & Koppel A G, Berlin-Drewitz
TR	Tanganyika Railway
UE	Usambara Eisenbahn
UR	Uganda Railway (period 1896–1926)
WD	War Department

BIBLIOGRAPHY

Bulman, W. E.   'The development of motive power on the EAR & H Administration', *Journal of the East African Institution of Engineers*, Vol 8 no 3 (1958), 82–93

——.   'Tanganyika trains', *SPEAR* Vol 5 no 6 (1961), 129–33

Cobb, T. H.   'EAR & H 1: the Kenya-Uganda Railway', *Railway Magazine*, April 1950, 262–7

——.   'EAR & H 2: the Tanganyika Railway', *Railway Magazine*, May 1950, 296–8

Carling, D. R.   *4–8–0 Tender Locomotives*, Newton Abbot 1971

Durrant, A. E.   *The Garratt Locomotive*, Newton Abbot 1969

Gauld, R. D.   'The Central Line of (late) German East Africa', *Railway Magazine*, December 1919, 375–80

Gibson, G.   'EAR & H 3: Kenya-Uganda Railway locomotives', *Railway Magazine*, June 1950, 398–405

Hill, M. F.   *Permanent Way*, 2 volumes, Nairobi 1949 & 1961

Ramsdale, R. S.   'The Uganda Railway', *Railway Magazine* 1904, 496–501

Sams, J. G. B.   'Train working on the Kenya & Uganda Railway' *Railway Magazine*, July 1932, 53–5

Schroeter, H.   *Die Eisenbahnen der ehemaligen Deutschen Schutzgebiete Afrikas und ihre Fahrzeuge*, Frankfurt/Main 1961

Smith, A.   'The Sigi Tramway that was: Tanganyika's railway development policy in the twenties', *East Africa Journal*, April 1968 20–6

——.   'The line of the wide horizon: Uganda Railway advancement', *Railway Magazine*, 1914, 172–3

——.   'named locomotives in East Africa', *Railway Magazine*, November 1954, 804

——.   'East African locomotive names', *Railway Magazine*, November 1955, 803–4

EAR   East African Railways locomotive diagrams (for internal use, unpublished)

——.   '*EAR named locomotives*', Nairobi, 1971 (brochure)

CREDITS FOR PHOTOGRAPHS

THE author wishes to express his thanks to the following for their kind permission to use their photographs:

Crown Agents, pp 34 (lower), 37, 43 (upper), 45 (upper) and 48 (lower).

East African Railways, pp 13, 21, 22, 29 (lower), 30, 31 (both), 33, 34 (upper), 35, 38, 42, 47, 48 (upper), 49, 50, 51, 53, 55, 56 (lower), 58, 59, 60, 63, 65 (lower), 68 (both), 69, 71 and 78.

F. Jordan, Nairobi, p 32.

The Mitchell Library, Glasgow, pp 28 and 29 (upper).

H. Schroeter, Bad Homburg, pp 18, 19, 20, 23, 24 (both), 25 and 26 (upper).

Photographs not acknowledged above are from the author's collection.

INDEX

Italic numerals refer to illustration pages